coriander

bay leaves

sweet marjoram

HERBS

tarragon

caraway seeds

dried tarragon

coriander leaves

garlic

sorrel

chopped parsley

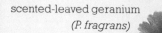

scented-leaved geranium
(*P. fragrans*)

lemon balm

vervain seeds

angelica seeds

tansy

pennyroyal

HERBS

A COMPLETE GUIDE
TO THEIR CULTIVATION AND USE

Ann Bonar

rose petals

marshmallow seeds

sweet cicely

marigold seeds

borage seeds

bergamot

rugosa rose hips

HAMLYN

4 | *Designed and produced by*
Nicholas Enterprises Ltd.
70 Old Compton Street
London W1V 5PA

Editor: Jennifer Mulherin
Art direction: Tom Deas/Rita Wuethrich
Illustrations: Sue Wickison
Special photography: Simon Butcher
Medical advisor: Dr Malcolm Stuart

Published 1985 by
Hamlyn Publishing
A division of The Hamlyn Publishing Group Ltd.
Bridge House, London Road
Twickenham, Middlesex

Printed in Belgium
ISBN 0 600 30619 4

Contents

Introduction

An informal herb garden of culinary herbs, including thyme and chives. The stone pedestal gives the garden a focal point.

The fascination of herbs is a powerful one and, once one is charmed, it is difficult to prevent them taking over one s life. They romp through the garden and take root in all sorts of unexpected places, they turn up in previously sedate and well-tried recipes, provide remedies for long-standing aches and pains, and have uses for the household and its pets.

The invasion is practically always a beneficial and harmless one – even stinging nettles have their uses as the invading Roman soldiery found when they tried to find ways of keeping warm in the chilly offshore islands of Britain. I said practically always, because a few herbs are harmful if used indiscreetly. In medically prescribed quantities such plants do nothing but good, but in amounts larger than these they can be harmful, even lethal. If a herb mentioned in this book can be poisonous, the fact is noted under its description in the alphabetical list.

Herbs are almost certainly more popular now than they have ever been, partly because a certain air of mysticism and legend surrounds them, gathered in the course of centuries, and partly because there is a tremendous surge towards using natural and unadulterated food and medicine, and towards ornaments and clothing hand-made from natural materials. Products synthesized in the laboratory, turned out on the factory bench, 'manufactured' in fast-food kitchens or fabricated from the by-products of fossilized fuels, are no longer universally acceptable. The herbal plant can supply substances, flavours, colorants and aromas naturally, often in combination with other ingredients which enhance their activity.

It must be said that the reputation which herbs have thus gathered is not unfounded. They can add a great deal to the flavour of food, and they do act effectively as anti-pest deterrents. A great deal of good for health, whether human or animal, is possible, and they are of considerable cosmetic and household use. In fact, we are merely at the beginning of the herbal turn-round – nine-tenths of the iceberg of herbal use has yet to be discovered, and it is only, even now, a small percentage of the population for whom herbs have everday use. The time is certainly coming when herbs will automatically be part of the garden or household stores, to be used daily in one capacity or another.

The history of herbs is an intricate one, reaching back to the most ancient civilizations, and accounts show that their herb usage still has relevance for us, even in our nuclear age. Indeed, a great deal can be learnt from such records, and it is well worth reading the ancient herbals which are currently in print.

The uses to which herbs can be put are described in some detail in this book, with tables to summarize these uses for quick reference. There are designs for herb gardens, and ideas for places to use herbs in the garden.

Growing one's own plants is the most satisfactory way to obtain the leaves, seeds, or whatever part of the herb is required, so information on cultivation is supplied. Many herbs are plants which are native, growing wild in fields and woods, and kept rigorously out of gardens, on the grounds that they are weeds. Others are plants introduced from overseas, often from warmer climates, which have nevertheless naturalized themselves in the countryside as escapes from cultivated areas and become weeds in their own right. So it is worth remembering before you conscientiously remove every last scrap of a 'weed' from a flower border, that it is more than likely to be of some considerable service. Horsetail may flourish like dragon's teeth, but its silicon content ensured that it did wonders for scouring out cooking pots, and it is said to be a collector of gold as well!

Not surprisingly, in view of the above, most herbs are easily grown, though there is generally some special need peculiar to each herb which must be catered for, to ensure satisfactorily healthy growth. Sometimes they need actual confinement of roots or climbing shoots. Difficulty is occasionally experienced with seed germination; herbs which flower and set seed in July-August often have a short viability, and need to be sown as soon as ripe, rather than in the following spring. Other methods of propagation, such as cuttings and divisions, are standard gardening practice, but whatever method of increase is suitable to a herb will be found in its description and specification in the alphabetical list.

The right methods of harvesting and preserving are important, and 'smell', whether fragrance or aroma, is discussed in a chapter of its own; it is one of the main attributes of herbs – for instance, it can be an attractant or repellent for many insects, beneficial or otherwise.

There is also a descriptive alphabetical list of 59 herbs, with notes on cultivation specific to each herb, its botanical characteristics and a 'recipe' which may be medical, culinary or whatever aspect is particularly appropriate to that herb. There are lists of herbs for special purposes and uses in the garden, and addresses of established herb gardens to visit.

Herbs past and present

Specimen page of pressed herbs from a nineteenth-century herbarium. The herbs are labelled with their botanical names and the dates on which they were collected. In the past, pressing was a popular and easy method of preserving plants and flowers and was used by both amateur and professional botanists.

Without plants man could not survive. Cereals (sophisticated grasses), fruits, vegetables, seeds and nuts are essential constituents of human diet – some may say the only suitable ones – and even the meat we eat comes from animals which themselves fed on vegetation in the shape of grasses and herbaceous plants.

Herbs and food

The plants lumped together under the umbrella name of herbs do not appear at first glance to be essential to maintain life, but it is now becoming apparent that this concept could be wrong, and that herbs are as necessary as oxygen, though the ingredients they contribute, such as minerals and vitamins, may only be found in minute quantities. The so-called culinary herbs, parsley, mint, basil and so on, all have characteristic flavours which enable them to be used in recipes of their own, or added to dishes to give a tantalizing piquancy. It is not always realized that often a herb will help with digestion generally, or with the digestion of the particular food with which it is associated. Peppermint is a classic aid to food absorption; basil contains a substance which helps with stomach cramps, and parsley is a diuretic.

The strong flavours of culinary herbs ensure that they should be used in small quantities, but there is no need to go to the other extreme and be timid with them. The Greeks strew their common thyme liberally all over roasted or kebabed lamb, to its great enhancement, and it is worth applying this principle to all the cooking herbs. The leaves are nearly always the part of the plant used, newly picked and freshly chopped at once, or used dried, provided they are no older than six months.

Aromatic herbs are the ones most used in cooking; no two are alike and some are so difficult to describe that even to say they are clove-like gives the wrong idea. The fact is that many have an aroma and flavour which is unique – for instance, basil can only be described as tasting like basil. Some are so strongly aromatic as to be spicy, and tarragon in particular is one of the few that has such a strong taste it does need adding in minuscule amounts to meat or fish dishes. Bay is another; one leaf is quite powerful enough for the average family casserole.

Quite why food and diet have become of such interest in recent years is for the social historian to discuss, but there is no doubt about the present popularity of culinary herbs. The history of the use of herbs in food is naturally bound up with the history of food itself. It is commonly thought that herbs were used chiefly to disguise the flavour of bad meat during the winter when there was no recently slaughtered beef or lamb to be had, or when food in general had started to go off. But there were perfectly good ways of preserving food without refrigeration, which were followed even more diligently than we do nowadays in the time of the deep freeze.

However, herbs have always been used to pep up the more blandly-flavoured foods such as fish, vegetables and cereals. Interestingly, religion had a considerable influence on herbal use in cookery, since the church authorities decreed the times when meat should be eaten, when fish only was the rule, and when there were fast days or fasting weeks. Lenten food was especially plain, and herbs, and spices as well, were used a great deal in such food.

Looked at from the other side, it should be realized that blandly-flavoured foods reduced the strong and exotic taste of many herbs, and this is where the secret of using herbs in cooking lies – to use herbs in such quantities that the strength of their flavours balances the strength and flavour of the food to which they are added. They need to blend as well; it is no good using a herb whose taste contradicts that of the dish to which it is being added.

Herbs and health

The rise in the popularity of herbs as medicinal remedies is less obvious but it seems to have come partly from a general dissatisfaction with synthesized drugs, as well as plastics,

artificials and chemicals – 'manufactured' articles of all kinds, which are being rejected in favour of substances naturally grown and formed by hand into the artifact required.

Herbally-based remedies of old, using parts of plants fresh or dried in simple infusions, poultices or decoctions, have been found to have great health benefits but, though their method of application is simple, their prescribing is not, since they have to be tailored not only to a given malady, but to the person concerned. The combinations which can be obtained for this are infinite. Further complications have to be added; for instance, various parts of a herb have different effects because the times of the year for collection affect the content of the herb; the quantity used is also of major importance, and there are at least 700 medicinal herbs used by European races! So, while herbs undoubtedly have marvellous potential for curing illness, home cures should only be undertaken for minor ailments.

The medicinal application of herbs can be traced as far back as a Chinese herbal written nearly 5,000 years ago, and there are Egyptian papyri from 2,800 B.C. listing such herbs as mint, marjoram and juniper for medicinal use. Much of the learning and practice of the Egyptians was absorbed by Greek physicians, one of the best known of whom is Dioscorides, an army doctor who lived during the time of Nero in the first century A.D. His list of 400 healing plants, described and detailed in four books, is probably the most famous *materia medica* of all, and continued to be a standard reference for European medicine for the next 1,500 years.

Plants were the only source of help for health improvement for hundreds of years, and doctors were almost entirely reliant on them though some, notably Hippocrates, did stress that hygiene and diet were of major importance. Medical men had perforce to be botanists, and often gardeners as well, and in time medical knowledge came to be the perquisite of the European religious orders, as it had been that of the priests in the time of the Egyptian pharaohs. For many centuries it remained in the hands mainly of the monastic houses, where there was always a physic garden containing the herbs required by the prevailing medical encumbent.

Most of the herbs now grown in Britain, culinary and domestic, as well as medicinal, resulted from the Roman invasion. In the same way, herbs were introduced in the sixteenth century from Europe to North America, to be grafted on to the use already in existence of the herbs of the North American Indians who had a considerable and long-standing tradition of herbal cures from the plants native to their own continent.

Medicine, while still based on plants, became more and more sophisticated as knowledge accumulated, especially with the introduction of printing, which meant that information could be passed on exactly, instead of inaccurately, by hearsay, and thus provided a bigger and bigger base from which to work. The Doctrine of Signatures became fashionable, the theory of which was that plants which looked like the symptoms of an illness would cure it – lungwort or pulmonaria is a case in point, since it was used for lung conditions, because its white-spotted leaves were thought to bear some resemblance to diseased lungs.

As the science of the nineteenth century advanced in analytical skills, it became increasingly possible to tie down results to specific plants and the chemicals therein, until a pure chemical could be prescribed for a particular symptom. The use of a whole leaf, flower or the entire plant itself, fell into disuse, and with this a whole galaxy of other chemicals

Frontispiece to the 1636 edition of John Gerard's *Herball*, first published in 1597 (**left**). Gerard, one of the most influential English herbalists along with Nicholas Culpeper (**below**), acknowledges his debt to the ancient botanists, Theophrastus and Dioscorides, by including their portraits on this frontispiece.

Right: Chamomile, a versatile herb, most commonly used to make a refreshing tea. The dried flowerheads can also be used to soften and lighten fair hair.

which, it has now been found, were equally necessary to a cure.

There seems no good reason why herbs should not be used at home to cure many minor ills, in the same way that aspirin are useful for headaches, toothache, etc., and the day may not be far away when a book of standard prescriptions using herbs is universally available. One will need to grow the plants and prepare the drink or poultice oneself, but neither is time-consuming, and certainly likely to be less expensive and just as, if not more, efficacious than the manufactured kind available from the chemist.

Herbs for the household
In the same way that there are now few modern savoury recipes that do not have herbs in them, and that more and more people are trying herbal remedies for aches and pains, so the uses to which herbs can be put for cosmetic and domestic purposes are being more widely explored. Lavender bags were not merely intended for perfuming household linen and blankets in the days of Elizabeth I – they acted as a deterrent to moths, fleas and other unwanted pests; and the stems were once burnt as a fumigant in sick-rooms. Oil of lavender rubbed into the skin will ward off mosquitoes and flies.

Herbs for beauty

Dyes for hair colouring could only be obtained from plants and one of the oldest of these is the red dye henna, obtained from the powdered dried leaves of the plant *Lawsonia inermis*. Traces have been found on the mummified bodies entombed in the pyramids of Egypt, and the plant's red colouring has been used ever since by various races and civilizations not only for hair, but also for nails and skin. Another plant much used for hair colouring is chamomile, the flower-heads of which provide a solution which lightens light-brown and fair hair appreciably; saffron will have the same effect.

The cosmetic uses of herbs are legion: skin cleansers, face-masks, shampoos, bath oils and salts, herbal soaps, talcum powders, and oils and creams. Women, and men for that matter, had no sources to call upon for improvement of their looks other than plants, and the vast cosmetic industry that we know today has replaced what was probably just as complicated a business two or three thousand years ago, given the great number of plants that have cosmetic application. Chinese ladies used perfume from plants for their hair, the Romans used herbs of all kinds, especially lavender, for bathing – even the ancient Britons used a plant for colouring their skins, the infamous woad, *Isatis tinctoria*, whose leaves, made into a paste, supplied a blue dye. According to legend, the ancient Britons painted themselves with woad to frighten their enemies but, almost certainly, this was not the only reason for so doing, since it is a styptic, i.e. it has the power to stop bleeding.

Herbs and dyeing

Man's increasing domestication meant he became more interested in the appearance of his home, and in the materials he wore to keep out the cold and wet. Edible plants that stained the skin while being prepared for eating, or being eaten, such as blackberries, would have been amongst the first to be tried for dyeing; gradually the range of colours available from plants increased by using combinations of dyes to take in every shade possible. The Chinese had dyeing down to a fine art as much as 5,000 years ago, and there are herbs grown today whose names record their colouring ability, such as dyer's-greenweed and dyer's-bugloss. Dye plants often have the word *tinctoria* as their specific epithet, from the Latin word *tinctorius*, meaning 'of the dyers'. Elder, *Sambucus nigra*, will produce dull blue, lavender and purples; marigold petals were once used for colouring butter and cheese, and the common dandelion supplies pink.

The Industrial Revolution saw the development of chemical dyes, as derivatives from side-products of coal-tar. The cheapness of the method, combined with the ease in ensuring that a particular colour would be identical in shade to the one used earlier, meant that plant dyes soon fell into disuse except in remote country areas. But although no two dyes obtained from plants will be exactly alike, the colours are soft and subtle, and the mixtures can be blended to give sophisticated hues and tints equal to any of the manufactured colourings.

Dyes in all the colours of the rainbow can be extracted from herbs, mainly by boiling or soaking the plant tissue. Standard quantities of plant and water are used in whichever method is adopted, for times of up to six hours, to take in the various stages required. In order to fix the dye in the material, a mordant, i.e. a chemical of some kind such as iron, tin, chrome or alum, must be used. These can be obtained from chemists. The material to be dyed is first thoroughly moistened and then placed in a solution of the mordant, simmered for a given period of time, about an hour, and then put, still wet, into the dyeing solution. Mordants will alter the shade or strength of a colour; for example, onion will produce yellow with alum, and dark brown with chrome. The most easily dyed materials are wool and silk; cotton and linen are difficult as they are made primarily of cellulose, being obtained from plants, rather than animal protein, and are better reserved for the time when experience has been obtained with dyeing wool.

Herbs and perfumery

Of course, one of the outstanding characteristics of herbs is what might be termed their nasal quality. The perfumes and aromas exuded by their leaves and flowers on a warm sunny day give any garden a fourth dimension, and one of the charms of the Greek and Italian hillsides is the pungently aromatic fragrance given off by the herbs and shrubs. Some herbs have scented flowers which can be smelt before the plant is seen; the apothecary's rose, *Rosa gallica officinalis*, is an example. Others such as rosemary (*Rosmarinus officinalis*) have leaves with a strong, sneeze-inducing odour; yet others have flowers or leaves which need to be rubbed in the fingers before the aroma can be enjoyed, such as lavender (*Lavandula angustifolia*), or ginger mint (*Mentha* x *gentilis* 'Variegata').

Perfumery is perhaps an even more ancient art than dyeing; it is a more obvious constituent of a plant, so would have been experimented with earlier, to disguise bad smells if nothing else, such as those of rotting meat and decaying vegetation. Fresh flowers are fine for scenting the air but their life is finite, and to preserve their perfume, it was found that a mixture of flower petals, collected when they were at exactly the right stage in their development, then carefully dried or part-dried, and mixed with an ingredient which 'fixed' the perfume, such as orris root (*Iris germanica florentina*) would continue to give off fragrance for months and even years. Such a mixture we now know as potpourri, from the French *pourrir*, to rot, not a very accurate name, since the ingredients are preserved rather than allowed to decay.

Eventually there came the discovery that a scented oil could be extracted from those flowers or leaves which were perfumed. Enfleurage is one method of doing this, by making a kind of sandwich with purified fat forming the 'bread', and the flower petals the contents of the sandwich. Distillation is another, in which flowers are boiled in water, and the

Above: Dyer's greenweed, a dye herb producing a good strong yellow, was used by both the ancient Greeks and Romans. Its flowerheads and seeds were also once used to treat rheumatism and dropsy, and as a purgative.

Opposite above: Culinary herb garden with bronze fennel, rosemary, tarragon and chives among other plants. Throughout the ages the most extensive use of herbs has been in cooking and for flavouring food.

Opposite below right: It was once thought that plants that looked like the symptoms of an illness could be used to cure it. Lungwort, for example, was recommended for lung conditions because people believed its white spotted leaves bore a resemblance to diseased lungs.

Opposite below left: The apothecary's rose, since early times source of some of the best known and most loved of all herbal perfumes, scented oils and waters.

essential oil given off in the steam is collected and condensed by cooling. Extraction with alcohol is a third method, when the solvent trickles over the plant material, is collected and then distilled to leave the oil as a solid material.

Fragrant herbs play a great part in what has come to be called aromatherapy, in which essential fragrant oils from herbs are rubbed on to the skin. The different fragrances are thought to have an improving effect on a variety of physical and emotional problems.

Now that herbs have invaded many parts of our lives, and not least our gardens, how much of this is just a fashionable phase, and how much will remain as a permanent and essential ingredient of everyday living? Since herbs do so much for the flavour of food and its digestion, have such profound use in medicine, both for humans and animals, and have so much utilitarian value domestically in the home, and in the garden, it seems most unlikely that they will ever fall into such disuse again. The countries of the Third World in particular need them desperately for medical purposes, as the synthesized drugs are so expensive. Another pointer to their continued and increasing use is the recent interest in holistic medicine, the philosophy of which can have such far-reaching effects that the entire way of life of modern civilization may be completely altered by the time the twenty-first century is well under way.

Cultivating herbs

A simple but attractive country-house herb garden designed around a stone statue. The plants include rue, fennel and comfrey.

Since no self-respecting modern cookbook leaves herbs out of its recipes, since courses in herbal medicine are springing up all over the place, and since cosmetics which rely on plants are taking the place of the synthetic beauty treatments what, one might ask, is a herb?

What is a herb?

Until recently, the word has always conjured up pictures of food, which imposed an artificial limit on the range of plants. Now that herbal usage has been revived so much in other disciplines, the definition has expanded to include plants usually grown nowadays for garden ornament, such as the Christmas rose (*Helleborus niger*), marigold (*Calendula*) and the Florentine iris; plants which were regarded as weeds, such as tansy, comfrey, yarrow and herb robert, but are being treated with respect as their usefulness for all sorts of reasons is realized again; and plants which supply dyes, cosmetics, insect repellents and fragrances.

Strictly speaking, a herb is any perennial plant whose soft or succulent stems die down to ground level every year, but many herbs are shrubs and trees, such as hyssop, the sweet bay and rosemary. A modern definition of a herb could be any plant, generally aromatic or fragrant, whose parts, whether leaf, flower, seed or root, are of use in food flavouring, medicine, household and cosmetics.

Herbs were, first and foremost, grown primarily for healing and flavouring and, as such, were grown in a place reserved for them, whether it was part of a monastery garden, or part of the vegetable patch of peasant or yeoman farmer. As times passed, inevitably, people began to arrange their herbs in patterns when they planted them, until eventually the herb patch became ornamental, and was a garden in its own right. The physic gardens of the monasteries were mostly formal, with rectangular or square beds, but the gardens attached to private homes were developed from these simple plans into intricate designs of curved beds edged with dwarf hedges of box, southernwood or lavender.

Propagation of herbs

Since 'herb' is an umbrella word covering all types of plant, it follows that they can be propagated by most of the methods used for plant increase, but there are two commonly used: seed and division. A third sometimes used is cuttings, mainly for the shrubs or trees. Most of the herbs which can be grown from seed are hardy and can be sown outdoors in temperate climates; some examples are dill, coriander, savory, purslane and lovage. Spring is generally the season in which to sow, but some germinate better if sown in late summer or early autumn, that is, as soon as the parent plants have flowered and set seed, and the seed has ripened. The seed of such plants loses its viability – ability to germinate – more quickly, so that a spring sowing is likely to result in fewer seedlings. Some seed should not be covered with soil because it needs light to germinate, some needs an acid-reacting soil, and some needs a period of cold between harvest and sowing. But most herb seeds germinate like weeds, not surprisingly.

Division is a second method which is probably more certain, provided the separated sections each have some root and some buds or potential shoots. It can be done in spring or autumn when the soil is moist, but not waterlogged or dry, and if it is still warm from summer, or beginning to warm up as the spring sun appears. Divided plants will take hold of the soil and grow new roots more quickly if they are replanted so quickly that the plant hardly knows it has been out of the ground. By doing this its vitality is not completely stopped, it somehow goes on flowing, and the plant, as it were, simply gulps a little, and gets on with expanding.

Nurseries and garden centres

Division is all very well, but you must first catch your plant, and in order to do this, it means applying to nurseries or garden centres. Local outlets of this kind will have a choice of all sorts of garden plants, and nowadays, a separate area is often reserved specially for herbs. Some garden centres make a point of having a particularly good collection of

herbs, and if they do, it will have well-grown plants, considerable variety, and correct naming. If there is such an outlet in the neighbourhood, it will be a more satisfactory source than a mail-order nursery, because you can see what you are buying, you can check that it is the plant as named on the label, and you can make sure of getting a strong healthy specimen free from pest or disease.

Moreover, the herb can be planted without disturbance to the roots, almost immediately after buying, whereas those sent through the post may spend many days travelling in inadequate packaging, having been dug up or removed from a container. Even plants which were well grown, and vigorous to start with, are unlikely to do well after such treatment, and unfortunately the mail-order nurseries have no control over postal treatment or delays. As far as cost is concerned, there is little difference between the two sources, since the cost of postage is offset by the extra cost of the container plants from a garden centre.

But it must be said that, even with the best garden centres, the range of herbs is not great, and consists mostly of the culinary type. For the widest selection, it is better to apply to a specialist herb nursery, of which there are now a good many. If there is a local one, then that is far and away the best place to go, otherwise there is no avoiding a postal order. A specialist nursery has the advantage that it can advise on the growing conditions in which the herb does best and advice may be available on the various ways of using it. Some nurseries run short courses on cultivation, cooking with herbs, perfumery and other uses.

As with any plant, when buying it, look for a specimen which is undamaged and healthy, and with plenty of potential growth in the form of small new shoots and buds. Avoid those with broken or hanging stems, wilting leaves, dry compost, any pest or leaf discolouration at all, and preferably buy a plant not yet flowering, though the buds may already be visible. Tall lanky plants in small pots are not likely to be a good buy. Be very careful if the herb has flowered and started to set seed, because if it is an annual, or a biennial, it will shortly die in the natural course of events. This is why it is worth finding out in advance what type of herb it is.

The correct naming of herbs is a third aspect which unfortunately is not yet as good as it should be. Mail-order plants that turn out not to be the ones ordered are tiresome enough, but when they are labelled as the plant ordered, and are not that plant, it is particularly irritating. Herbs to keep an eye on are the marjorams, of which there are at least three different kinds, tarragon (two), dill and fennel, which hybridize very easily, garden mint which is often a cross with horse-mint, or may even be that species, lovage which can look like ground-elder while young, and French sorrel which is invariably confused with the inferior-tasting English sorrel.

Besides mail-order herb nurseries, there are also seed firms supplying nothing but herbs and wild plants. These will be much less expensive on postage charges, and are more likely to be true to name. For success in growing from seed, there is a book entitled, *Seed Grower's Guide to Herbs and Wild Flowers* by Helen McEwan (available from Seed Bank, 44 Albion Road, Sutton, Surrey, England) which has detailed instructions on seed germination and seedling cultivation for herbs, together with information on their uses.

Left: Many specialist herb nurseries are planned so that the visitor can inspect the plants and their condition at close range. Each herb is labelled with both its botanical and common name.

Above: The leaf pattern of fennel is similar to that of dill. When buying a fennel plant, check that it is true fennel (*Foeniculum vulgare*) which has a strong anise flavour.

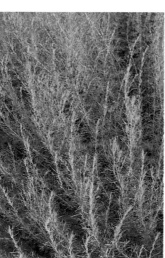

Above: Coriander is easily grown from seed but should be planted outdoors and not in a confined space. Until the seeds ripen, it has a strong and disagreeable odour.

French tarragon (*Artemisia dracunculus*) (**left**) is one of the most distinctive and delicious culinary herbs. Its close relation, Russian tarragon (*Artemisia dracunculoides*) (**far left**) has a greatly inferior flavour and should not be substituted in the garden, or the kitchen, for true tarragon.

Herbs in the garden

The use of herbs during the twentieth century had dwindled so much before their present popularity that it had been reduced to the culinary few, such as parsley and mint, with adventurous cooks experimenting with chives, sage and thyme. Consequently herbs were simply not part of the garden scene, being tucked away in an odd corner of the vegetable garden, or grown half-heartedly in pots or window-boxes, where they became aphid-ridden and dusty.

Now that herb nursery and seed lists name hundreds of species, the problem is not so much what to grow, as where to grow – how to fit as many as possible of these delightful plants into the general garden scene.

If the garden is small it will be a case of growing the monkey puzzle in the swimming pool, so many demands will be made on it, but most herbs are sufficiently ornamental to be fitted into the aesthetic need that a garden fulfils. They can be planted anywhere in the general scheme, mixed with herbaceous perennials, annuals, bulbs, shrubs or roses, provided the site chosen for them supplies their requirements, as with any garden plant. It is surprising how many herbs can thus be fitted in before that agonizing search for a space for yet another indispensable plant proves that the only vacancy is the concrete path surrounding the dustbins.

Sage, rosemary and lavender need no visual description, though it is not always realized that sage has spikes of vividly blue-mauve flowers which last a long time and are highly magnetic to bees. The thymes develop into nicely rounded dark evergreen bushes, also with the bonus of light purple, bee flowers; parsley leaves are perfectly acceptable as a foliage edging, chives supply a formal leaf silhouette, together with very desirable, long-lasting pinky mauve flower-heads, and so the list goes on.

Planting at random

Herbs distributed about the garden mixed in with the general plantings will often supply that 'surprise' quality that the old garden-landscape designers insisted on, as an aroma wafts through the air on a hot sunny day, or when a plant is brushed accidentally so that a spicy smell comes apparently out of nowhere. Not only that, it also seems to be true that certain herbs are good company for other plants, discouraging pests and diseases; for instance, chives and garlic have some ability to prevent roses being infected with black spot, and chamomile is said to improve the health of young plants if they are weak and slow to grow.

Growing herbs at random throughout a garden is in some ways the best arrangement – it is, after all, the way in which they would grow naturally – and species and varieties will be found that are happy on the rock garden, by the water, in bedding schemes, or as underplantings to tall perennials, shrubs and trees.

Herbs for mixed borders

Gardens which have been carefully designed and closely planted may appear to be unsuitable for additional plantings of herbs, but a herbaceous border, for instance, which needs to be re-dug every few years, with some of its encumbents divided or discarded, can well take some herbal plants, to supply flowers and/or architectural quality. Lovage and angelica are two tall, statuesque species with handsome leaves and flowerheads, needing the space provided by such a border. Bergamot (*Monarda didyma*) is a well-known border flower, which has all sorts of herbal attributes; the clove pink or gillyflower (*Dianthus caryophyllus*) is the highly scented forerunner of the modern garden pinks and border carnations, and its single-petalled, rosy purple or white flowers grow in clusters late in the summer. One can go on with example after example, whether the herb is grown for floral or foliage effect, and nearly all will enhance the appeal of the border, with their evocative fragrances and aromas.

One thing to watch for when buying herbs for the border; there are now garden forms of many herbs, or garden species grown in preference to the true herb. These are a different species, which do not contain as much of the herbal

essence, or may indeed not contain any. Catnip is an example; *Nepeta cataria* is the true herb and is the catnip that has a hard life if a cat is part of the household, but *Nepeta x faassenii*, also sometimes called catnip, is the usual species grown in gardens, with little if any attraction for cats, though it is always alive with bees when in flower. Another is goldenrod, *Solidago canadensis* and its derivatives being the garden forms, though the true herb is *S. virgaurea*, the native species, and much less tall-growing. Some garden herbs are variants of a species and are quite acceptable because they retain their herbal qualities. Examples are *Salvia officinalis purpurascens*, purple-leaved sage, ginger mint (*Mentha x gentilis* 'Variegata') with yellow-variegated leaves and blue rue (*Ruta graveolens* 'Jackmans Blue').

Herb borders

Herbaceous borders or mixed borders, or even the island beds of herbaceous perennials which make an interesting alternative, are a standard feature in many gardens, but few garden-owners take the word 'herbaceous' literally and grow nothing but herbs in their beds or borders. Such a border can be at least as ornamental as the conventional one, given the range of plants which are now considered to be herbs, and it is much more likely to be the haunt of bees and butterflies, as well as being more aromatic and fragrant.

A good many herbs have coloured leaves, and such plants can be distributed in the border to blend with the colours of flowering herbs and to provide a display when they are not in bloom. Golden-leaved marjoram, yellow-variegated lemon balm, white-variegated pineapple mint, purple-leaved sage, blue rue, the filmy leaves of bronze fennel, and the pink, purple and blue, leaf-like bracts of clary are a few herbs of this kind. It is also worth exploring the shapes of herbal leaves, such as those of lovage and angelica; chives, parsley, cotton lavender and rue are some more with contrasting and arresting foliage outlines. Carefully planted with adequate space and grown really well, it is possible to design a herb border which makes its point entirely with its foliage.

If flowers are preferred, it is a case of what to leave out, rather than hunting far and wide for attractive herb species. The reason for the rather dull image herbs have previously had is that most were grown to provide leaves for culinary use, and the flowers were of secondary importance; thyme and mint are typical. But herbs are also such plants as borage, honeysuckle, hyssop, marshmallow, yellow gentian, and evening primrose, all plants with beautifully coloured showy flowers, some for shade and some for sun.

The herb border can be designed to follow the same principles as those used for the herbaceous or mixed border; small plants will not thank you for planting them next to towering or buxom plants – they will be smothered in no time. In fact small plants really are better as edgings, at the front or round the perimeter of the bed. A pleasant cottage-garden effect can be obtained by random planting without regard to colour, or plants can be placed so that the colours of the flowers blend and combine. The trouble with this is that, although the plants are meant to bloom at the same time, invariably some flower later or earlier, and ruin the whole carefully thought-out scheme. Beds or borders of a width such that the centre is at arms' length from any point on the edge will be easier to maintain, but if this makes them too narrow for your choice, stepping-stones in the border make life a lot easier and incidentally add to the border's appearance.

Enthusiasm can spur one on to cram the border full of as

Medicinal herbs such as mullein, tansy, lovage and southernwood form a border under the shelter of a wall.

Annual herbs
BASIL
BORAGE
CHERVIL
CORIANDER
DILL
FENUGREEK
MARIGOLD
MARJORAM, SWEET
MUSTARD
SAVORY, SUMMER

Herbaceous perennials
ANGELICA
BALM, LEMON
BERGAMOT
BURNET, SALAD
CATMINT
CHAMOMILE
COMFREY
COSTMARY
DANDELION
FENNEL
FEVERFEW
HORSERADISH
HORSETAIL
LOVAGE
MARSHMALLOW
MINT
NETTLE
ORRIS ROOT
PENNYROYAL
PINK
SWEET CICELY
SORREL
TANSY
TARRAGON, FRENCH
VALERIAN
YARROW

Shrubs
BAY, SWEET
COTTON LAVENDER
ELDER
HONEYSUCKLE
HYSSOP
LAVENDER
LEMON VERBENA
ROSE
ROSEMARY
RUE
SAGE
SAVORY, WINTER
SOUTHERNWOOD
THYME

many herbs as possible, but some of them are likely to die as a result, and others will be tall and weedy; it is far better to plant with spaces between them to start with, allowing them room to grow to their full size so that their growth habit and leaf value can be made the most of in the context of the overall design. As with any border, plants with evergreen or evergrey leaves make it more interesting in winter, so consider this backbone first, and include such plants as sweet bay, southernwood and rosemary.

Herbs for walls, pavings and patios

When space is at a premium, don't forget that paving and free-standing dry stone walls or double low brick walls will provide niches for all sorts of the smaller herbs, especially those native to areas where there are long hot summers following comparatively mild rainy winters such as the Mediterranean. In fact, such sites can be made a feature in the garden, and it could be worth building a wall on purpose, which would form a barrier to cold wind and contain warmth on its sunny side.

Patios lend themselves in particular to herb cultivation because they are so often sited next to the house and facing the sun. The house walls store heat and provide a shelter from the winds that can be even more damaging than frost, so that double walls can be planted to thyme, rosemary, tarragon, sage and lemon verbena. Plants which have very aromatic leaves are delightful to plant in such areas, as the hot sun helps release the aromatic oils, and the fragrant air which results adds another dimension to the pleasure of eating or sitting outdoors. Cistus (rock rose), scented-leaved pelargoniums (geraniums) and the curry plant (*Helichrysum angustifolium*) are a few that can be combined to provide the mixture of aromas reminiscent of holidays in southern Europe.

When preparing double walls for permanent plantings of this kind, a height of about 45 cm (18 in) and an internal width of at least 15 cm (6 in) will provide internal space for sufficient compost to grow the small herbal shrubs and perennial plants, and allow good drainage in the base. The hard core footing alone will automatically take care of most of this aspect, but it is advisable to put a finer layer over it of shingle and then gravel about 5 cm (2 in) deep, and then fill the remaining space with a soil-containing compost of the John Innes No 2 type (see pages 38–39). This will need topdressing each year in spring, together with the addition of a little slow-acting organic fertilizer – herbs are much more aromatic when grown 'hard' with little nutrient.

Walls built to support terraces, used as boundaries, forming part of a flight of steps, containing raised beds and so on, whether brick or stone, lend themselves to planting actually in their fabric. Feverfew, soapwort, chamomile, wallflower and clove pinks are some to plant in crevices and holes in the wall itself, first putting in a little compost for the plant's roots to get a grip on. If the space extends to soil at the back of the wall, so much the better, as the plant can then root through into it, and the choice widens to include any small perennial herb.

Formal paved areas in the garden provide a nice contrast to the freely curving growth of the plants but, however well laid the paving stones, tiles or bricks, sooner or later weeds sprout through the cracks, and it is either a case of weedkiller, not popular with organic gardeners, or constant weeding, which scrapes fingertips and breaks nails. Some of this can be prevented by deliberately planting the joins with herbs like creeping thyme (*Thymus* x ·*serpyllum*) and

Top: Here feathery fennel is attractively positioned against the window of a small conservatory.

Above: Angelica and cotton lavender are just two of the herbs growing in this mixed border beside garden steps.

Right above: A small oval herb garden has been created on this patio. Behind is a raised bed of flowering plants and climbing roses.

Herbs for planting amongst paving
CHAMOMILE
CHIVES
FEVERFEW
MARJORAM
PENNYROYAL
THYME, CREEPING

For hedges
BAY, SWEET
COTTON LAVENDER
ELDER
LAVENDER
ROSE
ROSEMARY

For edging
BURNET, SALAD
COTTON LAVENDER
HYSSOP
RUE
SAGE
SAVORY, WINTER
SOUTHERNWOOD

pennyroyal (*Mentha pulegium*) which have matted stems lying flat on the ground. They smell delicious when walked on. Chives will grow in such a situation, and their narrow, tall shape does not take up much room even if it is vertical. Feverfew, nasturtiums and chamomile will also seed themselves between the cracks but at this point one can be back to the weeding situation and the paving loses its character of precision and smoothness.

Herbs in containers

The paved surfaces of patios and terraces can in fact be rather daunting in their bareness, and a little relief is easily supplied in the shape of plant containers. Something will be found for every style of house and garden, and every kind of planting. Many, many herbs are first-class in containers like these, and one can have the pleasure of a spring display, to be replaced by summer-flowering fragrant herbs, all with a permanent backbone of evergreens such as lavender, sweet bay, cotton lavender, or rosemary.

Where the climate has frosty winters, containers enable the tender herbs to be grown through the summer so that they may be dried and preserved for use in winter, or kept growing in the greenhouse or home. Some will survive winter outdoors with plenty of lagging round the container so that the roots do not get frozen, and protective mulches, or plastic sheet round the top growth.

Ornamental herbs for the terrace could consist of mixtures of catmint, old-fashioned marigolds (calendula species), the Florentine iris, jasmine, wallflowers, basil – the purple-leaved kind – *Rosa gallica officinalis*, blue-leaved rue, and the ever-greens referred to above. Besides their decorative qualities, all these can be used for either cooking, medicine, as perfumery, or domestically.

Containers also come into their own for convenience, or for would-be gardeners without a garden, but with an area, balcony or roof-garden. In particular, the kitchen herbs are liable not to be used unless they are very close to hand for the cook; in the rush of making up food amongst all the other demands being made at the same time, a trough or window-box of herbs on the kitchen windowsill or just outside the backdoor will ensure that culinary herbs are used daily. Some of them will be permanent, such as sage, thyme, the mints, chives, bay and rosemary; parsley will need sowing annually, so will sweet marjoram and basil, neither of the last two being hardy. For more exotic kitchen herbs, choices are amongst dill, coriander, chervil, and the savories, winter and summer.

Whatever container is used, always provide good compost, and try to give the plant plenty of root room. The plants from countries with hot dry summers tend to put their roots down very deeply into the soil, especially if they are growing in rocky soil on exposed hillsides, so containers with as much depth as possible are advisable. Vigorous plants such as the mints, horseradish (grown for its roots), and sweet cicely need plenty of root room. Parsley needs far more root-room than it is usually given; the main or tap root is rather like a small carrot, and this should be allowed for. The alternative name for a close relation, Hamburg parsley, is turnip-rooted, the root being the part for which it is grown, and ordinary parsley tends to follow the same root pattern.

One point worth remembering about the management of plants in containers; they need watering, and in summer usually very frequently – daily if they are in pots and the weather is hot – so it pays to have as large a container as possible. Plants will use proportionately less water and save time, with the bonuses that plants do better with company, and damage to the roots from frost in winter is less likely.

Designing your herb garden

Cotton lavender forms the hedges in this knot garden at the chateau of Chenonceaux in France.

From a herb border to a complete herb garden is not a very long step, and once the initial interest has been started with the planting of single plants here and there in the garden, it is not long before friends are giving one new species, other varieties are discovered at garden centres, and catalogues are found to list even more. Lists from specialist herb nurseries arrive, many of which give names of herb gardens in their neighbourhood open to public viewing, and so the idea of one's own herb garden begins to take shape.

It can be as large or as small as you want it – a stately-home herb garden with grand borders, 'knotted' beds, paving, pergolas and a pool with goldfish (or carp, to be in keeping with the true tradition of the old monastery herb garden). Or it can be a modest affair of three or four small beds with a sundial in the centre, chamomile paths and parsley edgings.

Traditional knot garden
Whatever the size, formal and repetitive patterns are typical of, and necessary to, herb gardens. They provide unity, and help to give the planting coherence and shape, without which herbs tend to get out of hand, and look wild and woolly, especially towards the end of the season. The original monastery physic gardens were fairly plain, with rectangular or square beds in lines, but as time went on, and private households began to grow their own medicinal cures, food flavourings and fragrances, the sites devoted to herbs became more elaborate, until they were often laid out in the 'knot' style, an intricate arrangement of beds said to have taken its name originally from the lover's knot.

But the knot pattern had to be precise to get its maximum effect, so the beds were all outlined with small neat hedges – in other words edgings, such as clipped dwarf box, southernwood or hyssop – and the paths between, if not chamomile, were raked gravel or small coloured pebbles. This style is, of course, ideal for containing herbs and formalizing them; to be truly knot-like, however, all the plants should be low-growing, so that they can be looked down upon, and the intertwined pattern clearly seen. Such designs should repeat within the confines of the herb garden, and the plants in the beds should be the same in corresponding sites in other beds. These also help to tie the whole arrangement together, but in a small herb garden it is too restrictive of plant species, and one can still get a good result if individual beds are planted with different collections.

Knot-garden patterns were highly advanced, somewhat geometrical, and needed a great deal of care in laying out on the site, and then planting. Considerable skill in getting plants established was also required – it is only too easy for gaps to appear, or for an odd man out in flower colour to pop up, as anyone who has ever tried to grow a complete row of vegetables or lay out a bedding plan, will know. Indeed, the knot gardens must have been the forerunners of the Victorian bedding schemes which have equally elaborate designs, the differences being that they relied on colour for their main effect, and also often reproduced an object or spelt out words.

Points to consider before designing your herb garden
In designing and planting your own herb garden, it should take account of various factors such as:

Your purpose in having a herb garden
Do you want it to be attractive to look at, a place to sit and be peaceful? Is it to provide herbs for use, such as flavouring herbs, medicinal herbs, or household and insecticidal herbs? Must it provide fragrance and a haven for butterflies, and a happy hunting-ground for bees? Are you going to concentrate on collections of herbs each with a theme?

The soil and site
It is no good trying to grow plants unsuited to the soil and aspect. They will be a continual disappointment as they fail to leaf, flower or set seed, become pest-ridden, and need constant attention. Decide on your herbs, and then find out

what kind of soil they need – moist, heavy and deep, or dry, well-drained and short of plant food; also whether they do best in sun or a little shade, with shelter, or exposed to some wind, and whether they are immune to cold, or need cosseting and protection.

The amount of money you have to spare
If money is tight, you can get plants as gifts from generous friends; even just cuttings will turn into plants, or collect wayside seeds or seedheads, but not plants (remember there are Wildlife Preservation Orders in force in most countries). You can acquire some most unusual species for a song at village jumble sales, country fetes, and street markets. Many herbs grow easily from seed, fortunately still reasonably inexpensive, and you can save seed and take your own cuttings from year to year.

The amount of time you have to spare
The time spent on the herb garden is probably less than on any other part of the whole garden (unless it has been deliberately planted to be labour-saving), but shortage of time is less of a problem than money, since the herb-garden is a hobby, undertaken for enjoyment and relaxation. In any case most of the time required will be taken up at the beginning, in the planning and drawing out of the plan on paper, in choosing the plants, and in soil preparation and planting. Paths with whatever surface is chosen can be laid at the start when the beds are being dug or later at a more convenient time, but it does make life easier if they can be finished before planting the beds.

What herbs to grow

Next to the difficult decision as to which of many enchanting patterns or knots to draw on the soil with herbs, is the even more difficult but absorbing one of which species to grow. Since there are hundreds, it is a job for those long winter evenings of which, in theory, there should be so many. You can plant a random collection without any motif, simply growing herbs which particularly appeal to you, or you can assemble collections which have a theme, rather like stamp collectors who concentrate on stamps of the Caribbean or the early triangular stamps of the African countries.

The utility aspect is an obvious one, both for interest and for practical help in itself – cook's herbs, cosmetic herbs, medicinal herbs, dye herbs, household herbs – any of these groups could include at least ten different species. The collection could consist entirely of culinary kinds; the health-giving species can lead to a very large collection, as four, five or six different plants may be needed to make up a prescription. Dye-producing herbs include some unexpected plants, such as elder (blue from the fruit) and stinging nettle, which produces a warm brown. The dye garden may look as though it is full of weeds, but most of them are only wild plants under another name. If you accept the definition of a weed as 'a plant growing where it is not wanted', once it has a use and is being grown for a purpose, it is no longer a weed.

On the other hand, although a herb garden grown entirely for its fragrances and aromas does little to conserve the environment, it will contain such plants as the scented roses (the more strongly perfumed they are, the better) – the damask rose (*Rosa damascena*), and the cabbage rose (*R. centifolia*); also lavender; lily-of-the-valley; jasmine (*Jasminum officinale*); and border pink (*Dianthus caryophyllus*). Surprisingly, scented lilies are not used to supply perfume

The centrepiece of this rectangular herb garden is a circular pond around which the herb beds are arranged. This is one of the simplest and most attractive designs for a small herb garden.

Herbs grown from seed
BALM, LEMON
BASIL, SWEET
BORAGE
CARAWAY
CATMINT
CHERVIL
CLARY
CORIANDER
DILL
ELDER
FENNEL
FENUGREEK
FEVERFEW
LOVAGE
MARIGOLD
MARJORAM, SWEET
MULLEIN
MUSTARD
NETTLE
PARSLEY
SAVORY, SUMMER
SAVORY, WINTER
SWEET CICELY
SORREL
WALLFLOWER

Herbs grown from cuttings
BAY
COTTON LAVENDER
DANDELION (ROOT)
ELDER
FEVERFEW
GERANIUM, SCENTED-LEAVED
HONEYSUCKLE
HORSERADISH (ROOT)
HYSSOP
LAVENDER
LEMON VERBENA
ROSE
ROSEMARY
RUE
SAGE
SOUTHERNWOOD
THYME

because it cannot be extracted from them successfully. The aromatic herbs such as basil, lemon verbena, myrtle and pelargonium can also contribute a lot to the garden's beauty.

But collections of herbs can be grown purely for interest's sake. For instance, collecting botanical families of herbs, one to a border, will reveal that the *Labiatae*, *Umbelliferae* and *Compositae* are the ones containing the most herbal plants at present in use in Europe and North America. The rose family (*Rosaceae*) comes a close second and the *Scrophulariaceae*, of which mullein and eyebright are members, is another. Herbs mentioned in the Bible make another interesting collection, so do those which Shakespeare brings into his plays, particularly as they give an authentic picture of plants used by the Elizabethans – poor, mad Ophelia's flowers included rue, fennel, rosemary, violets, a daisy and some pansies, all good herbs, even the daisy, which was once called 'bruisewort'.

If you are not a bee-keeper, you may easily become one by amassing herbs beloved by bees and/or butterflies; many herbs are bee plants such as goldenrod, mullein, honey-suckle, thyme, catmint and bergamot. Or you can collect herbs into beds of different colours: yellow, with woad, evening primrose, dandelion, tansy and golden marjoram; blues, to include sage, borage, hyssop, alkanet, clary and rosemary; and white flowers – jasmine, sweet cicely, the Florentine iris, myrtle and lily-of-the-valley.

Herbs of a similar colour can be effective when planted together. Golden marjoram, variegated lemon balm and feverfew are the plants used to create this 'golden corner'.

Planning and planting a herb-garden

Every good garden design book advises the would-be designer-gardener to 'first take your squared paper' and, in fact, it is a good idea to draw the plan to scale. The size of the beds is much more easily appreciated, the spaces between them can be better compared to the dimensions of the beds, and the proportions of the various plants can be correctly assessed, so that mistakes in juxtaposition can be adjusted. Better still, if you are anything of an artist, is then to transpose your scale plan to a three-dimensional drawing, preferably coloured, showing it as it will be in three or four years' time when the perennial plants are mature.

Steps in designing

1 Assess your soil:

Is it well-drained (sandy, shingly, gravelly, chalky)?

Does it hold water and feel sticky when wet, cracking badly when dry (predominantly clay or silt)?

Is it dark-coloured, spongy when wet and dusty when dry (peat)?

How does it react to a pH test (acid or alkaline)?

Does it contain organic matter (material floating on the surface of a solution of soil)?

2 Assess your site:

Which parts are sunny/shady?

Does it get wind, if so, where from (north, south, east or west)?

Is it likely to retain frost and collect snow in winter?

Is it sheltered by walls/fences/hedges?

Is the garden close to the sea?

What is average winter and summer rainfall?

Where does the water lie the longest?

3 In the light of answers to these questions, choose your herbs. Whatever choice of herb you settle on, before you start to mark the places for them on your paper plan, make sure you know what their final size will be when they are mature. The adult height and width are important facts, armed with which you can plant without crowding or spacing; if the soil is a well-worked heavy one, allow for extra growth. The converse is seldom true, since many herbs grow naturally in poor dry soils.

4 Make a rough diagram of your design and determine whether it is appropriate to the size of the site, e.g. a herb border on the grand scale will not be successful in an area 3 × 3 metres (10 × 10 ft); in other words the proportions of the design should be such that there is room to make the most of them in the area concerned.

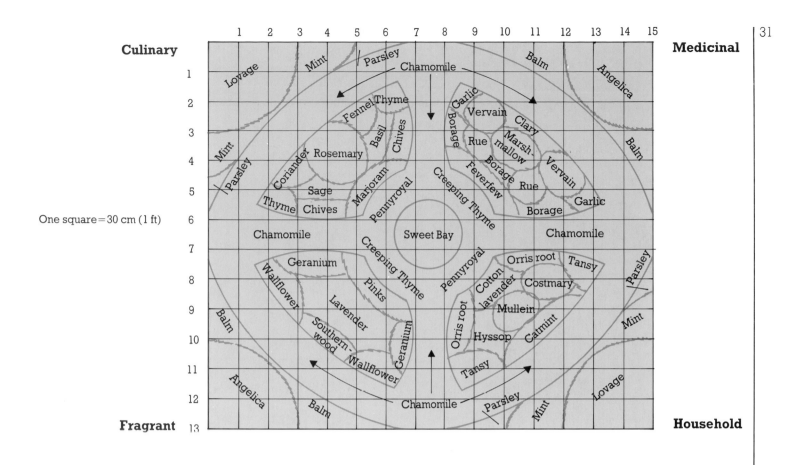

5 Choose your plants according to your needs and the dictates of the soil and site as determined from your assessment.

6 Enter their name on the diagram in your preferred arrangement, taking into account height as well as spread, whether they are evergreen, perennial, annual, flowering or non-flowering.

At this stage, it can help to trace the design on the site in outline with the help of chalk, rope, string, or the garden hose, and to use canes stuck in the soil to give an indication of the final height of plants.

7 Measure the area exactly and scale it down for transfer to squared paper – a large scale would be 1.2 cm (½ in) per 30 cm (12 in), but if you want to mark in all the plants in all the beds, it would have to be of the order of 5 cm/30 cm (2 in/12 in).

8 Mark in the beds and borders on it to the dimensions required, in the required positions.

9 Write in the names of the plants where they fit in to the pattern and draw a circle round them to indicate the extent of their final spread.

10 Decide on the numbers of plants and the seeds required, and order accordingly, unless you are planning to plant up from various sources.

The diagram above is a herb garden containing a collection of herbs grown in Britain and on the Continent in mediaeval times; they have a variety of uses, and some of them fulfil several functions.

Notes to the above
The tall plants have been put at the back of the beds or in the centre; plants which are low-growing have been put near the edges, and naturally dwarf shrubs have been used for the edging, which gives the beds the necessary precision and unites the pattern. The pattern is further emphasized by repetition of plantings. Herbs with evergreen leaves continue to provide a structural pattern in winter and cover the ground to some extent, though in a herb garden it is never possible to have a permanent blanket of vegetation if you wish to grow the annual herbs such as summer savory, coriander or sweet marjoram. Sun-loving herbs are placed in the centre; aromatic plants are distributed throughout the pattern to provide aromas and fragrances. A good deal of use is made of leaf quality, though with showy flowers e.g. tansy, marigold, feverfew, chives, rue, borage, clary and mustard.

Herbs which need cooler soil, depth and permanent moisture should be planted in a position likely to provide this, so a site near the boundary to the south provides shade and is less likely to dry out. The mint should have a place where it can be easily chopped out before it runs amok amongst its neighbours. Feverfew will seed itself enthusiastically, so will borage, and parsley, where it is happy.

Herbs grown by division
BALM, LEMON
BERGAMOT
BURNET, SALAD
CATMINT
CHAMOMILE
COMFREY
COSTMARY
FENNEL
FEVERFEW
MADDER
MARSHMALLOW
NETTLE (RUNNERS)
ORRIS ROOT
PENNYROYAL
PINK
SORREL
TANSY
TARRAGON
THYME
VALERIAN
VERVAIN
YARROW

Care of herbs

Most herbs grow well in a sunny, sheltered site. A south-facing wall offers ideal protection, especially against wind which can be damaging to sensitive herbs.

The plants grown in gardens are all indigenous to one country or another, whether it is Britain, Italy, China, or in North America or South America. Some of them have been got at by the plant-breeders and bear no resemblance to the species or variety originally discovered; some remain the same, being already sufficiently beautiful or useful.

Some are difficult to grow under cultivation because of their natural habitat's different climatic, soil or aspect requirements, but some grow like the weeds they often are in their native land.

The plants grown as herbs in many countries have been used by the inhabitants because it was, and is, natural to use the materials found in the world around one for food, shelter, health and warmth. Once sown or planted, herbs will grow strongly and healthily to maturity in the majority of cases without help, except while seedlings or young plants, but even so the help needed will be minimal. You can, of course, spend time on their care; working amongst herbs in a herb garden is a particular pleasure to which fragrance, nostalgia, usefulness and the anticipatory satisfaction of one's stomach all contribute. On a warm, sunny day, when the bees and butterflies are working amongst the flowers, and your fingers are releasing the aromatic oils into the atmosphere, tranquillity and contentment unavoidably seep into one's outlook.

Site and soil

However, it does pay to provide some care and attention when growing herbs in the mass, to ensure their greater decorativeness and well-being, or even simply to curtail the activity of the lustier wild plants. It is frequently said that most herbs do best if they are growing in well-drained soil, somewhat short of plant food, and in a position which is sunny and sheltered. However, this is a generalization which really does not apply, any more than it does to all garden plants. There are certainly some, the Mediterranean group for example, which includes oregano, lavender, rosemary and thyme, that grow in this sort of environment, but there are many more which need such conditions as shade, moisture, plenty of food, or deep soil, or they may want varying combinations of these, or any of them combined with their opposites. Parsley does best in deep moist soil and sun; the mints prefer the same soil, and are impervious to shade or sun, but pineapple mint will survive in drought much better than ginger mint.

Really, to give each herb the best possible chance, the site and soil chosen for it should conform to its specific needs, as with any garden plant. Having said that, it is possible to plant some in groups, and it is true to say that some thrive in soil which would normally be considered unsatisfactory.

A position which provides shelter from wind is almost more important than one which receives all the sun available; wind is excessively drying and moisture is transpired from plants much more quickly than is realized, along with the essential oils, relatively 'heavy' though they are. Frost pockets, i.e. places where frost remains during the day when other parts of the garden have thawed, should be avoided, also soil where water stands in winter, but these are all qualifications applicable to general planting.

Preparing the soil

Provided the soil is workable, a spit (spade's length) deep and not violently acid or alkaline, it will need little preparatory treatment. Complete removal of weeds, including all the roots, is important, preferably by hand or while digging; incidentally, do remember that some of them may be the very plants you are intending to grow, though if the area contains horsetail it is better not to try growing perennial plants in it until you have been clearing out this weed for some years.

Dig the soil to the depth of a spade or fork, and clear out the rubbish as you go – large stones, glass, china, bottle tops, sticks, wire, plastic and so on – at the same time mixing in a thin layer of rotted garden compost, especially if the soil is shallow and only a few cm (in) deep on top of chalk subsoil.

Seeding and planting: (1) Sieve fine soil onto the seeds. (2) Cover the seed tray with glass and paper to keep out the light. (3) When the seeds have sprouted use a fine mist spray to keep the soil moist. (4) Plant the seedlings so that the stem is buried up to the lowest leaves.

Transplanting (1) Carefully remove the herb plant from the pot. (2) Very gently loosen exposed roots. (3) Plant in the soil ball so that the top is just below ground level. (4) Firm the soil around the plant.

There are not many herbs which prefer acid soil, so if your soil is acid use chalk (calcium carbonate) or ground limestone (the same substance but less quick-acting) to alter it to a depth suitable for adequate root growth. Quantities should be of the order ½-1 kg per sq m (1-2 lb per sq yd) where the pH is 6.0, and double this if it is 5.0, giving less for sandy soil and more for clay.

The pH of a soil, though it sounds mysterious and scientific, is simply the name for the scale which determines the quantities of chemical particles (hydrogen ions) contained in the soil solution, more or less of which make the soil acid or alkaline. Soil tests to discover the pH are easily done, and the kits for doing them are provided with instructions by several garden product companies, and stocked at garden shops.

Do this initial cultivation in early spring, and be ready to hoe or fork out weeds again once or twice more before planting or sowing in mid-spring, as weed seeds will germinate more readily when the soil is disturbed, and with the start of warmer weather. At the same time, if the soil is one of those obviously dry, gritty or chalky ones, from which the minerals plants need as part of their food – potassium, magnesium, nitrogen, etc. – have been washed out by rain, mix in slow-release fertilizers. Bonemeal is a good base which lasts several years, and can be spread at the rate of about 180-240 g per sq m (6-8 oz per sq yd), and garden compost into which wood ashes have been mixed is particularly helpful on such soils.

Sowing and germination

For successful seed germination, it is absolutely essential that the soil surface is of a fine consistency. All the best books advise that the texture should be like fine breadcrumbs, and this is literally the state it should be in. Sowing seed amongst lumps of soil, even if they are only 6 mm (¼ in) in diameter, will not result in seedlings – the seed simply does not germinate, however much you water the soil and protect it from cold.

Once the soil has been dug, it should be broken up with a fork, hoe, back of a rake, by hand, with a hand fork, or whatever you find most convenient, until it reaches the stage at which raking it backwards and forwards, and then crossways, reduces it to the fine tilth described. If you have the time to do it, tread the soil after the breaking-up stage but before raking it. This will help the seedlings to get a better hold, and will make it evenly firm – this in turn results in even germination, without gaps.

Whether you then sow the seeds in rows, or in patches, or in 'stations' – groups spaced several cm (in) apart – is up to you; in any case, some herbs do better sown in boxes or a seedbed, and then transplanted; others are better sown where they are to grow and then thinned. Whatever you do, try to sow into moist soil, when rain is expected, and the temperature rising; put a thin covering over the seed, between 3 and 6 mm deep (again there are exceptions to this, noted in the descriptive list), firm it, and water every evening with a fine spray of water if there is no rain. Get rid of weed seedlings before they become young plants, and thin the herb seedlings when they are large enough to handle to about 6 mm (¼ in) spacing, and when they have filled this, to their final spacing. A row about 100 cm (3 ft) long is ample for one family's needs for most herbs.

Some herb seeds germinate best soon after they ripen in summer, and should be sown towards the end of summer, though with packet seed this is not always possible. However, a spring sowing of such seed will produce some plants, though the number will be fewer than from a summer sowing.

Herbs can be started from small plants; planting in spring is again the most convenient time. If they came from a garden centre, take the container off each root-ball, cut any long,

In very dry weather, some herbs will need watering. A garden hose with sprinkler attached will do this most efficiently.

Stem cuttings: First make a clean cut immediately below the leaf joint straight across, so that the cutting is 7.5-10cm (3-4in) long. Remove lower leaves so that none are buried in the compost. Then insert the cutting at the side of the pot to a depth of half of its length. Keep the pot moist and out of direct sunlight until the cuttings are ready for planting out.

coiled-round roots off level with the soil-ball, and plant without otherwise disturbing in a hole sufficiently deep to ensure that the surface of the soil-ball is level with or a little below that of the surrounding soil. If the plants are bare-rooted, spread the roots out in the hole, with the same proviso regarding the long ones, and then crumble soil in over them to fill the hole. Make them firm in their place, and water them unless the soil is really wet, or heavy rain is imminent. Space all of them appropriately for their final size, and put in stakes wherever support may be needed.

Routine maintenance
Once herbs are in place, and you have ensured a good start to their lives with properly prepared soil and the right planting technique, there is little more to do. Weeds may get in the way early on and should be dealt with before they swamp your seedlings and small plants – the smaller they are when hoed off, the quicker and easier it is to do it. Tie tall plants to their supports as they grow, and break off the tips of the main shoot of plants you want to be bushy, just above a leaf or pair of leaves, when they are a few cm (in) tall; basil, rosemary, hyssop, marjoram, mint, sage and savory are some of these. Sideshoots can thus be treated as well. Some shrubby herbs may need further pruning during the summer.

In very dry weather, and light soil, some of them will want watering, not just a watering-canful, but a prolonged sprinkling with a spray attachment from a hose for about half an hour. Moisture loss can be prevented with a covering of compost on the soil surface (mulch), and by mixing compost in during the initial digging each spring. Good garden compost will prevent the appearance of weeds in the first place, though badly-made material which has not heated up well will still have live weed seeds in it.

Pest and disease control is virtually unnecessary. If plants have anything wrong with them it may have already been there when they were obtained, or it is a sign that they are not being grown in the right conditions. Some plants are prone to a particular disease or pest: rust infects mint, greenfly infests parsley during drought, and slugs and snails will eat many seedlings.

Preparation for winter
In autumn when the plants have begun to die down naturally the perennials should have their flowered stems cut off at ground level, if not already done, and annuals should be dug up and put for compost. The herb beds should be lightly dug over with a fork, weeded if necessary, and the invasive plants chopped back at the roots. Old perennial herbs should also be dug up, and only the youngest parts, at the edge of the crown, replanted. This dividing technique is a useful method of increase, and works well, provided each piece has some root and some dormant buds or young shoots.

Some herbs which are tender can be dug up and planted in containers during early-mid autumn, first cutting off their no-longer-wanted top growth. New shoots will already be appearing at the base of many herbs, and marjoram and mints respond well to this treatment.

In particularly cold winters, when frost is prolonged or there are bitter north-east winds, some herbs will be killed; thyme, sage, rosemary, marjoram, tarragon and pineapple mint are examples. Soil which is waterlogged for weeks at a time will make matters worse, and can even kill plants without their first being weakened by cold. You can take cuttings in summer of this kind of herb and keep them protected through the winter, or shield the parent plants in some way, so that they are sheltered from the worst of the cold and wind. Cloches, straw, plastic sheet, pads of wire netting with straw or bracken between them, sacking or conifer branches all provide shelter and will keep off the worst of the weather.

Herbs in containers

For containers	
BASIL, SWEET Provence pots	PINKS Troughs
BAY, SWEET Tubs	ROSEMARY Tubs
BURNET, SALAD Pots, troughs	RUE Urns, stoneware
CHAMOMILE Troughs	SAGE Troughs, urns
CHERVIL Troughs	SOUTHERNWOOD Tubs
COTTON LAVENDER Urns	SORREL Pots, troughs
FEVERFEW Troughs	TARRAGON Large pots
GERANIUM, SCENTED-LEAVED Pots	THYME Troughs, pots
LAVENDER Tubs	**Herbs for hanging baskets**
LEMON VERBENA Tubs	BASIL, SWEET
	BORAGE
MARIGOLD Pots, troughs	BURNET, SALAD
	FEVERFEW
MARJORAM, SWEET Pots	MARIGOLD
	MARJORAM, SWEET
MINT, GARDEN Large pots, buckets	MINT
	PENNYROYAL
PARSLEY Pots	PARSLEY
	THYME
	WALLFLOWERS, DWARF

Herbs are one of the best groups of plants to grow in containers on the whole, as they mostly take very kindly to this form of cultivation. Some are annuals or biennials, many are compact perennials or subshrubs; even the sweet bay, a tree, can be grown satisfactorily in a tub. Some are even better for it – the mints, horseradish and lemon balm are examples – otherwise they invade their neighbours and strangle them. Container growing is convenient, too, in that herbs can be protected in winter, the containers can be put where most convenient or most suitable for the herbs, and they can be used for decorating otherwise austere sites such as paving, basement areas and concrete yards.

Container herbs outdoors

Troughs outside the kitchen can be filled with chives, marjoram, thyme and sage in one trough, and parsley, mints, borage, French sorrel and lemon balm in another, depending on space available. The first one is a 'hot' box, the second a moist, deep one, good in partial shade.

Formally clipped bay-trees trimmed into shapes as balls, pyramids or cones look superb outside front-doors or as eye-catchers on a terrace or patio; rosemary can serve the same purpose, and in a smaller way, so can rue, lavender, sage and cotton lavender. Tubs suit the bigger specimens best; terracotta Provence pots and urns, the ones that are shatter-proof in frost, have a gorgeously warm look, and seem to be the natural home of this kind of shrubby aromatic herb.

Corners of the garden which are awkward and difficult to plant decoratively because of their size and soil state, could be successfully filled with a container-grown herb or herbs, even changing the display as the seasons alter. Marigolds, tansy, feverfew, golden marjoram and dill would all combine, in cultivation as well as colour; another mixture could be pinks, cotton lavender, blue rue, clary and borage. For a cool shady corner which gets sun at some time during the day, comfrey, sorrel, costmary, alkanet and chervil would do well,

and for perfume, the container could include *Rosa damascena*, pinks, mignonette, honeysuckle or jasmine, and wallflowers, herbs which release their fragrance into the air.

For those who live in flats or apartments and have no gardens, containers will be the only possible way to grow herbs, but concrete or paved basement areas, flat roofs, window-sills and balconies can be oases of green all year with containers full of herbs, whether they are pots, boxes, tubs, gro-bags, urns, hanging baskets or sinks. The climbing plants are particularly effective and useful as they cover the vertical surfaces and make use of a third dimension. Privacy can be ensured, and warmth collected, in the shelter they provide.

Types of containers

The display can be even more eye-catching if use is made of the wide choice of containers now available. Anything goes, from redwood timber boxes and troughs, to highly sophisticated and decorated lead urns, cisterns and tanks. Bowl-like concrete planters enhance such herbs as wallflowers, followed by chamomile, mignonette, cotton lavender, and dill or fennel for height. Lead urns are elegant with trailing jasmine, catmint, rue and lavender; clay parsley pots could alternatively have small plants of feverfew pushed into all the openings, to flower all summer.

Expanded polystyrene pots and window-boxes, copper containers, space-age cylinders, stone urns and stone or wooden tubs, half barrels, sculptured terracotta clay from Italy and Provence, plastic and fibre-glass troughs – there is no end to the variety of size, shape, colour and texture for containers. The formality of the container itself gives herbs the precision they need to make the most of their subtle colourings and aromas, and to display their foliage shapes at their best.

Container herbs indoors

Herbs can be grown indoors in the house, on suitable

Gro-bags are particularly effective for many herbs such as basil, seen here flourishing profusely in this type of container.

window-sills, but they should receive as much light as possible, even those that like a little shade in the garden. The reason for this is that a window provides light only on one side; the other three sides and the top consist of the walls of the room and its ceiling, and the loss of available light is considerable. Only if the window is a sunny south-facing one should they be shaded a little during the middle of the day in summer when the sun is shining.

Space to grow plants will be in short supply indoors, but satisfactory quantities of culinary herbs can be grown; fragrance is possible, from mignonette, pinks and jasmine, and household or medicinal herbs of the smaller species could find a place, too: chamomile, hyssop, rue and vervain are examples. Such herbs can be grown in containers right from the start, or they can be dug up from the garden. If the latter, this should be done in late summer or early autumn, when the main summer growth has flowered and is beginning to wither, but new shoots are just appearing at the base of the plant. The old growth should be cut right off, to ground level, and the plant dug up with the main mass of roots as intact as possible. The long ones can be shortened to bring them into line, and broken ends tidied up by clean cutting. Then put the whole root-ball into a container which will take it without cramping, and which already has compost in the base, then fill in with compost at the sides. It should be watered well and allowed to drain, and then put into its place in the home, out of the sun for a day or two.

The new growth already appearing will lengthen quickly, and fresh leaves and shoots should be available for most of the winter. Even if the plants die down in mid winter, they will sprout again in spring earlier than if they were planted outdoors. One or two need to be kept on the cool side, otherwise they grow too fast and weaken themselves so badly that they die.

Composts and fertilizers for container herbs

Composts for herbs in containers do not have to be elaborate mixtures, and the prepacked soilless kinds whose bulk is peat and sand, or those containing loam such as the John Innes mixes, are excellent. For those herbs which have an especial liking for dry, quick-draining root environments, extra coarse grit or even small shingle can be added, e.g., add 1 potful of grit to 8 similarly-sized potfuls of soil compost. Soilless composts will do very well as they are, keeping them slightly on the dry side, but be very careful, as such composts take a long time to dry out but then do so completely with alarming rapidity, and are exceedingly difficult to wet through to the centre of the root-ball. John Innes compost can be made at home, according to the following formula:

> 7 parts loam   (all parts by volume)
> 3 parts granulated peat
> 2 parts coarse sand

Add to 1 bushel/8 gallons (36⅓ litres) of this mixture:

> 21 g (¾ oz) chalk
> 112 g (4 oz) base-fertilizer

Make up the fertilizer as follows:

> 2 parts superphosphate   (all parts by weight)
> 2 parts hoof and horn
> 1 part sulphate of potash

This provides John Innes potting compost No. 1. For successively larger and stronger-growing plants, use J.I. No. 2 or 3, which contains twice and three times as much respectively of chalk and fertilizer. If the mix is to confirm to the J.I. formula, the loam should be sterilized.

Soilless composts can also be put together at home, as in general they consist of 75 per cent granulated peat and 25 per cent fine sand; the amount of plant food and chalk in the proprietary kinds varies from brand to brand, and you can add your own as required, though a good general mixture can be obtained by adding about 28 g (1 oz) general fertilizer and 28 g (1 oz) chalk to 1 bushel/8 gallons (36⅓ litres) (by bulk) of compost, mixing all the ingredients thoroughly.

Cultivation and care of container herbs

Planting in pots and other containers calls for simple though necessary techniques to get good results, and these vary a little depending on whether the container is clay (or stone), or plastic of some kind, and on which type of compost is being used.

For clay and similar materials (but not plastic containers), cover the drainage hole with a broken piece of clay pot, convex side upwards – broken brick, rubble or expanded polystyrene pieces will also do – and fill in a little compost over it. Position the plant in the centre of the pot so that its crown is about 2 cm (1 in) below the pot rim (1 cm/½ in if the compost is soilless), spread the roots out if they do not already form a compact ball with the soil and, holding the plant with one hand, fill in compost with the other all round the roots until the pot is full. Firm it down with the fingers well, if it is John Innes compost, but compress it only lightly if soilless. Add a little more if necessary and tap the container on the working surface to shake the compost level, or use your hand lightly. Water the plant well and keep warm and shaded for a day or two while it settles down.

If containers do not have any drainage outlets, cover the base with at least 1 cm (½ in) depth of drainage crocks, shingle, etc. Plants that do not need repotting can be topdressed, that is, the top 2 or 3 cm (inch or so) of compost removed, to avoid injury to the roots, and replaced with new compost. Plants being potted on – removed into larger containers – can be taken out of pots, by up-ending them, and knocking the rim on the working surface, at the same time putting the other hand under the plant across the compost surface so that the root-ball falls out on to the palm of the hand. Large plants and containers make this impractical, and it is then a case of loosening the soil-ball at the sides with a stick pushed down against the inside wall of the container. A well-watered plant is easier to shift, and will suffer less.

Water requirements

Gauging water requirements is less difficult now that moisture meters are available, but in the absence of one, water to fill the space at the top of the container between compost surface and rim, let it soak through, repeat and allow the surplus to drain off, then leave the plant until the compost surface appears dry. Be careful with soilless composts – they have a nasty tendency to become bone-dry in the middle, while the surface remains moist and apparently well watered. Their weight is a good guide to the water content, and if the plant seems to be demanding water constantly and wilting frequently, then a thorough soaking is probably necessary, in a bucket of water or with a sprinkler left on.

Dealing with pests

There is little to do to container-grown herbs during their growth any more than there is to their open-ground counterparts. The removal of yellowing, withering or otherwise discoloured leaves keeps them looking their best; likewise faded flowers and flower stems. Tying to supports and some pruning will be needed by the climbers, to keep them in the space provided, and occasional spraying for the odd pest might be necessary. Greenfly and leafhopper are the most likely, usually when plants are not being watered enough, or are being starved, or grown in containers which are too small. Caterpillars can be handpicked; whitefly dealt with by using bioresmethrin. Red spider mite infestation is a bad sign, of poor cultivation and wrong conditions. It is difficult to deal with, so start again with new plants and different care in a different site. Scale insects can be handpicked, if found before they become an epidemic; follow hand removal with thorough washing down, and spraying with a soap solution.

Container herbs from soft cuttings

Apart from the method of division, herbs can be grown from cuttings, rooted in pots or boxes, and from seeds, usually sown in pans (shallow pots), or small seed-boxes. Tip or soft cuttings taken in early midsummer are the easiest to root; they consist of the tip of new shoots which are still lengthening, and are 5-10 cm (2-4 in) long. Each should be cut cleanly just below a leaf joint, and the lowest leaf or leaves removed completely, including the leaf stem if any. Put the cutting into a plastic bag at once, to retain as much moisture as possible in the leaves, unless you can pot it immediately. Use a proprietary cuttings compost, and fill a 9 cm (3½ in) pot to within 6 mm (½ in) of the rim, using drainage material, then put three or four cuttings spaced evenly round the side of the pot and, if there is room, one in the middle. Put the cuttings in to half their length, and make sure they are fairly firm, and the base of the stem is in contact with the compost, and water them in lightly. Put them in a propagator, or cover the pot with a plastic bag supported by split canes, and secured with a rubber band round the pot rim, and keep warm, 18-27°C (65-80°F), and shaded. Rooting will occur within one-three weeks in most cases.

Taking semi-hardwood and hardwood cuttings

Semi-hardwood cuttings are taken in mid to late summer, when the new season's shoots have begun to harden and turn woody and slightly brown on the outside. Such cuttings should be between 5 and 15 cm (2-6 in) long, and can be the end of a main shoot or part of a sideshoot, the tip in each case being still green and soft. They are prepared and potted in the same way as soft cuttings, but occasionally a variant is used if the plant is less easy to root. In such a case, a sideshoot is always used and is literally torn off the parent stem so that a sliver or 'heel' of bark and inner tissue is still attached to the cutting. There is then more surface area from

Formally clipped bay trees can look distinctive outside front doors, or on a terrace or patio.

which roots can be produced.

When tip, semi-hardwood or heel cuttings have produced roots, they should be transferred to individual pots, about 5-9 cm (2-3½ in) diameter, depending on the amount of root growth, and potted in the normal way to grow into small plants. They can then be planted outdoors or in containers, depending on the herb and its hardiness.

Hardwood cuttings are taken in autumn when the new shoots have become mostly hard and woody all along their length, except for the tip. They should be between 23 and 30 cm (9-12 in) long, with the lower leaves removed, and then buried for up to between half and two-thirds their length in a sheltered bed or border, spaced about 15 cm (6 in) apart. Soil for rooting should be reasonably friable and well-drained, and free of weeds; a little coarse sand in the base of the hole will help in rooting.

Leave the rooted cuttings where they are until the following autumn and, if well-rooted, transplant to their permanent positions, otherwise leave until the following mid spring.

Container herbs from seeds

Seeds are similarly sown in a special seed compost; the John Innes seed compost consists of:

> 2 parts loam   (by volume) preferably sterilized
> 1 part granulated peat
> 1 part coarse sand

to 1 bushel/8 gallons (36⅓ litres) of which mixture is added 21 g (¾ oz) chalk and 42 g (1½ oz) superphosphate. The mixture should be put through a 6 mm (¼ in) mesh sieve.

Containers should be filled to within 1 cm (½ in) of the rim and firmed down evenly – this is important to ensure even germination. Compost should be moist throughout. Seed is sown thinly and regularly on the surface, and covered with a thin layer of fine compost, unless otherwise noted in the descriptive list of herbs (pages 44–113). The container itself is then covered with black plastic sheet, or glass and brown paper, and put in a warm place, as with the cuttings. The compost should be moistened if it begins to become dry and, when germination occurs, the covering should be removed at once, and the seedlings kept in good light, but out of scorching sunlight. Thin them as they grow, and then transplant them (prick out) 5 cm (2 in) apart each way into boxes of potting compost, and finally plant them where they are to grow when they have filled the space available. Tender herbs should be gradually accustomed to lower temperatures before planting outdoors, and in any case should not be subjected to frost.

Identifying herbs

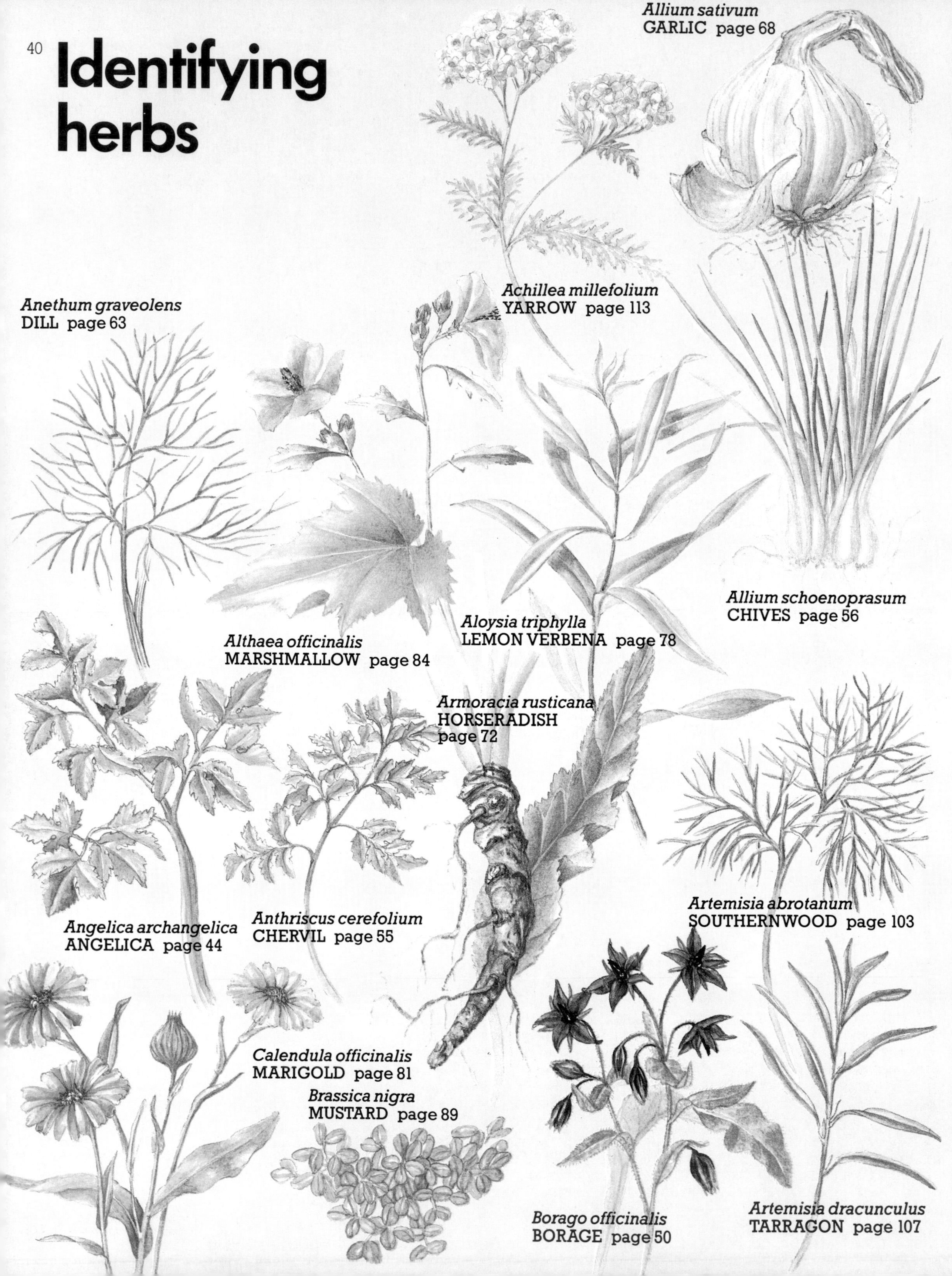

Allium sativum
GARLIC   page 68

Achillea millefolium
YARROW   page 113

Anethum graveolens
DILL   page 63

Allium schoenoprasum
CHIVES   page 56

Althaea officinalis
MARSHMALLOW   page 84

Aloysia triphylla
LEMON VERBENA   page 78

Armoracia rusticana
HORSERADISH
page 72

Artemisia abrotanum
SOUTHERNWOOD   page 103

Angelica archangelica
ANGELICA   page 44

Anthriscus cerefolium
CHERVIL   page 55

Calendula officinalis
MARIGOLD   page 81

Brassica nigra
MUSTARD   page 89

Borago officinalis
BORAGE   page 50

Artemisia dracunculus
TARRAGON   page 107

Carum carvi
CARAWAY page 52

Chamaemelum nobile
CHAMOMILE page 54

Cheiranthus cheiri
WALLFLOWER page 112

Chrysanthemum balsamita
COSTMARY page 60

Equisetum arvense
HORSETAIL page 74

Coriandrum sativum
CORIANDER page 59

Chrysanthemum parthenium
FEVERFEW page 67

Dianthus caryophyllus
PINK page 96

Foeniculum vulgare
FENNEL page 65

Hyssopus officinalis
HYSSOP page 75

Iris germanica florentina
ORRIS ROOT page 91

Lonicera periclymenum
HONEYSUCKLE page 71

Levisticum officinale
LOVAGE page 79

Lavandula angustifolia
LAVENDER page 76

Laurus nobilis
SWEET BAY page 48

Mentha pulegium decumbens
PENNYROYAL page 94

Melissa officinalis
BALM, LEMON page 45

Mentha spicata
GARDEN MINT page 85

Monarda didyma
BERGAMOT page 49

Ocimum basilicum
BASIL page 46

Origanum majorana
SWEET MARJORAM
page 82

Myrrhis odorata
SWEET CICELY page 105

Nepeta cataria
CATMINT page 53

Pelargonium spp.
SCENTED-LEAF GERANIUMS
page 70

Petroselinum crispum
PARSLEY page 92

Poterium sanguisorba
BURNET page 51

Rosa gallica officinalis
APOTHECARY'S ROSE page 96

Rumex acetosa
ENGLISH SORREL page 104

Rubia tinctorum
MADDER page 80

Rumex scutatus
FRENCH SORREL page 104

Rosmarinus officinalis
ROSEMARY page 98

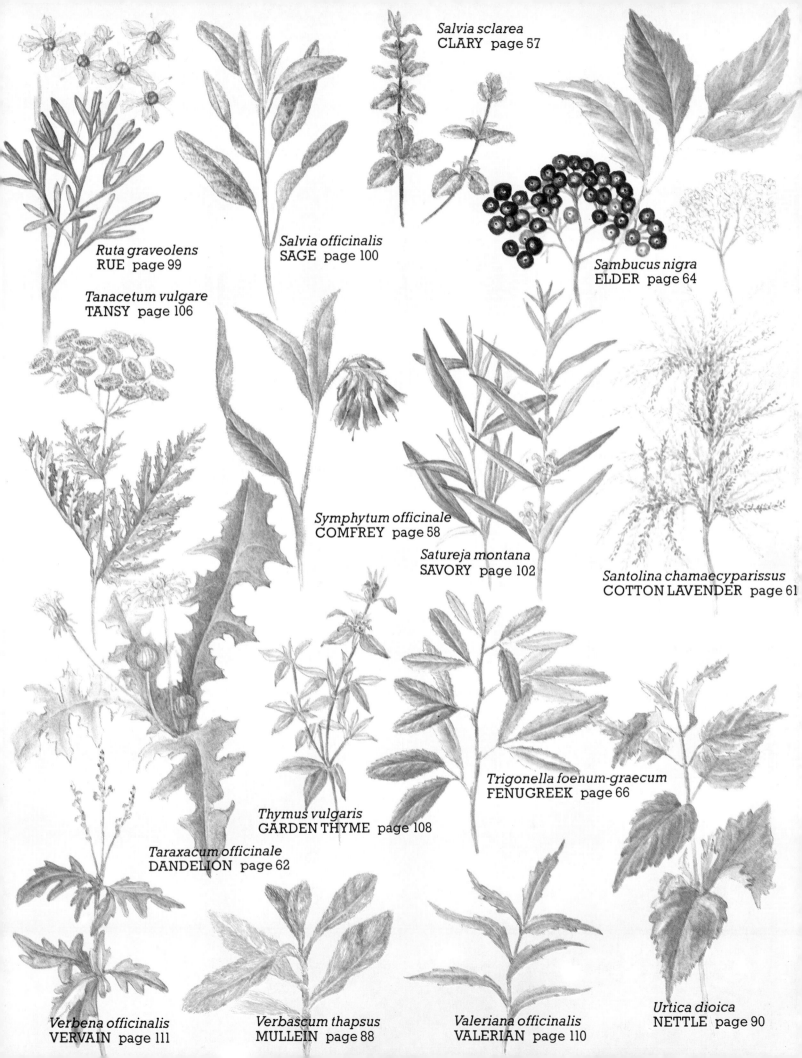

Salvia sclarea
CLARY page 57

Ruta graveolens
RUE page 99

Salvia officinalis
SAGE page 100

Sambucus nigra
ELDER page 64

Tanacetum vulgare
TANSY page 106

Symphytum officinale
COMFREY page 58

Satureja montana
SAVORY page 102

Santolina chamaecyparissus
COTTON LAVENDER page 61

Trigonella foenum-graecum
FENUGREEK page 66

Thymus vulgaris
GARDEN THYME page 108

Taraxacum officinale
DANDELION page 62

Urtica dioica
NETTLE page 90

Verbena officinalis
VERVAIN page 111

Verbascum thapsus
MULLEIN page 88

Valeriana officinalis
VALERIAN page 110

IDENTIFICATION

Height 1.2-1.8m (4-6ft), spread 75-90cm (2½-3ft)
Root long, thick and fleshy, yellowish grey; can weigh 1.3kg (3lb)
Stem hollow, ridged, stout, green to purplish
Leaf two to three-pinnate, up to 90cm (3ft) long, bright green, each leaflet toothed; leaf stalks sheath the stems
Flower yellowish green, tiny, in rounded clusters forming an umbel, July-August
Seed pale yellow when ripe, up to 6mm (¼in) long, ribbed on one side. Entire plant pleasantly aromatic including roots, reminiscent of musk or juniper

Angelica

This is one of the most ancient of herbs. Its modern use, in the form of the candied stems as a cake decoration, is a pathetic remnant of its former important role throughout everyday life, when all parts had their uses. Native to Northern Europe including Britain, it was possibly used in association with pagan festivals and was considered a protection against the evils of witchcraft. After Christianity was introduced, it acquired its name because it was likely to flower on or around May 8 in the old calendar, the feastday of Michael the Archangel. In Scandinavia the root used to be eaten as bread, and the strongly-flavoured seeds had all sorts of applications especially to alcoholic drinks. It grows in temperate regions of North America. The root is best dug for use in the first autumn after permanent planting.
Cultivation: Grow from fresh seed newly ripe, sown thinly in late summer-autumn in moist, deep, fertile soil and sun or shade. Transplant in spring or thin to 45cm (18in) apart, and plant in permanent site in autumn 90cm (3ft) apart. Flowering may occur in first summer, but is more likely in the second one; if flowers removed before seed set, plant will continue to live. Seed will self-sow. Can also be sown in spring, but germination rate low, or increased from offsets.

USES

Culinary candied stems for cakes and confectionery; seeds for flavouring a variety of drinks including vermouth, gin, Chartreuse and some white wines; leaves in stewed fruits and for flavouring cheese and cheese dishes, including cheesecake; should not be eaten by diabetics
Medicinal fresh leaf stems, seeds, of use in respiratory conditions such as colds, bronchitis and coughs; a stimulator of appetite and a digestive, not much used at present; dried roots anti-flatulent
Cosmetic virtually none
Domestic virtually none
Fragrance and Aroma whole plant, particularly root, pleasantly aromatic; seeds strongly flavoured and oil of angelica extracted from them, sometimes used in perfumery and potpourri

RECIPE

Candied angelica stems
Use young stems or leaf stalks; cut up into short lengths, simmer them in a little water until tender, then remove the tough outer skin, and simmer again until bright green. Dry and weigh, use an equal weight of sugar, sprinkle this on to the stems in a shallow dish and leave for two days. Then boil the mixture, drain, make more syrup in the same way and re-boil the stems for about 10 minutes. Remove and spread out to dry on a rack in an airy place; if not thoroughly dry, it becomes mouldy later – then store in airtight containers between greaseproof paper.

candied angelica stems

angelica seeds

dried angelica root

angelica root & leaves

dried angelica leaves

Balm, Lemon

Balm used to be one of the most important herbs in the garden, as it is a strongly bee-orientated plant. In fact, it was said that a plant of balm in the garden would ensure that the bees never left their hive to set up home elsewhere, and since sugar was highly priced in mediaeval days, honey carried a considerable premium.

A Middle-Eastern plant, balm is now naturalized in many cool temperate countries especially Europe and North America. It grows into a bushy plant, with soft leaves which smell strongly of lemon when bruised, delightful if planted at the side of a path. There is a yellow-leaved form, and a third with yellow-flecked leaves. Melissa tea has calming and soothing effects, relieves tiredness and helps headaches.

Cultivation: Once in the garden balm will always be present unless determined efforts are made to eradicate it. It will seed readily and spread, but established plants are not difficult to uproot. The rounded leafy plants do best in fertile, moist soil with some sun and shade; in poor dry soil they become small and straggling. Sow seed outdoors in spring, or divide the plants in spring, and allow 60cm (2ft) between plants. The stems die down in autumn and the crown may need protection in hard winters.

USES

Culinary fresh leaves for summer drinks and fruit cups, as tea and tisane, in jam, milk puddings, salad dressings, or as a substitute for grated lemon peel in a recipe
Medicinal fresh leaves, for headaches, calming nerves, inducing sleep, and easing insect bites
Cosmetic leaves to perfume soap, and as an astringent for the skin
Domestic in furniture polishes, for strewing and in water for laundry
Fragrance and Aroma leaves lemon scented, used in potpourri

RECIPE

Mushroom salad
100g/4oz/¼lb chopped mushrooms
1 lettuce
4 sticks celery chopped small
2 tbls fresh chopped lemon balm leaves
50g/2oz/½ cup cheese, grated finely
2 chopped apples
a little finely chopped onion
salt
little chopped sweet red pepper
Mix apples, mushrooms and salt with celery and onion. Place on a bed of lettuce, sprinkle cheese and a little chopped sweet red pepper over the top, and garnish with lemon balm leaves.

LABIATAE *Melissa officinalis*
Herbaceous perennial

45

IDENTIFICATION

Height 45-90cm (18-36in), spread 38-60cm (15-24in)
Root fibrous, spreading, tough, tenacious
Stem square, tough at the base, green, erect, branching, slightly hairy
Leaf green, heart-shaped, wrinkled, round-toothed, 6-7.5cm (2½-3in) long, 2.5-5cm (1-2in) wide, opposite
Flower white, 2-lipped tubular, 1.5cm (½in) long, in clusters on spikes July-September, inconspicuous
Seed brown-black

dried lemon balm leaves

lemon balm seeds

lemon balm leaves

mushroom salad

Basil, Sweet

India is the home of this strongly aromatic plant where it is perennial, and where its history of use stretches back many thousands of years. It is regarded as sacred by the Hindus and was much used for disinfecting where malaria was present in the house. From there it spread through Asia Minor to Greece and Rome, and thence to northern Europe and North America. A leafy bushy plant, much branched, Culpeper in the 17th century wrote of it as the 'herb which all authors are together by the ears about, and rail at one another like lawyers'. The strong and distinctive flavour of the leaves is certainly one which either makes enemies or gains lovers – there is no in-between.

Cultivation Basil does not transplant well, so seed is sown one or two to a small pot, and then planted out complete, without disturbing the root-ball. Sow seed in gentle heat early May and plant out early June. Plenty of sun and well-drained soil are essential; water well at midday in dry weather, pinch out tips of shoots regularly to prevent flowering. In containers sow in warmth in March and grow on in 15cm (6in) pots. Seed should only just be covered, and will turn blue after sowing.

Besides the plain green form, there is a purple-leaved kind, 'Dark Opal', decorative for a patio, and others smelling of fennel, lemon, or tarragon.

IDENTIFICATION

Height 90cm (3ft), spread 45cm (18in)
Root white and mainly fibrous, thin
Stem square, green, becoming tough
Leaf thin, bright green, entire, opposite, 2.5-5cm (1-2in) long, half as much wide
Flower white, small, two-lipped and tubular, in long spikes July-October depending on time of sowing
Seed black, tiny

spaghetti with pesto

dried basil leaves

basil seeds

fresh chopped basil

basil leaves

USES
Culinary fresh leaves with tomatoes, mushrooms, egg dishes, sausages, stuffings, sauces, chicken, French dressing and many meat dishes
Medicinal fresh leaf mildly sedative, and of use for stomach-ache and sickness; antiseptic
Cosmetic none
Domestic repels flies; once used for strewing, so probably repels fleas as well
Fragrance and Aroma pungently aromatic, somewhat of cloves, still used in perfumery

RECIPE
Pesto
This classic Genovese sauce, made with fresh basil, is served with pasta and soups. In southern France, where it is known as *pistou*, it is often an accompaniment to roast lamb.
50g/2oz/1 cup fresh basil leaves
25g/1oz/¼ cup pine kernels
2 cloves garlic
3-4 tbls olive oil
50g/2oz/½ cup freshly grated Parmesan, sardo or pecorino cheese
Pound together the basil, garlic and pine kernels in a mortar or blender until you have a fine paste. Add the grated cheese (which should be Parmesan alone or mixed with sardo or pecorino) and blend well. Gradually add the oil stirring steadily until it is amalgamated and the sauce has the consistency of a creamed butter.
   Made in larger quatities pesto can be preserved in jars if it is tightly packed (no air pockets should remain) and covered with a layer of olive oil. Seal and store in a cool place.

preserved pesto sauce

Bay, Sweet

The sweet bay is an evergreen shrub or shrubby tree from southern Europe and Asia Minor, whose leathery leaves are pungently aromatic and form the basis for much classic French cooking; bouquet garni has many variations, but a bay leaf is essential. Venerated by the Greeks and Romans, dedicated to Apollo and formed into leafy crowns for poets and triumphant generals, sweet bay is the source of the term 'bachelor' for academic honours, from the Roman *bacca laureus*, laurel berry. The French term *baccalaureat* for examinations is an even more direct derivation. Bay's chief use is in cooking, but it has some medical value also.

Cultivation Bay trees are planted in spring, in a sunny, sheltered place, and average, preferably well-drained, soil. Growth rate is slow, about 23cm (9in) a year; no particular care is needed, though any broken or dead shoots and branches should be removed at the end of winter; young plants will need protection in severe winters until well established. They do well in tubs, and can be clipped formally into various shapes, such as ball, pyramid, cone and so on, doing this training in late summer. Increase is by heel cuttings in early-midsummer under cover with a little bottom heat.

IDENTIFICATION

Height average 7.5m (25ft), in cool temperate conditions 4.5m (15ft); width 1.5-2.1m (5-7ft)
Root spreading, fibrous and anchoring, brown covering
Stem tough, woody, dark grey bark on trunk and branches
Leaf leathery, dark green, entire, pointed-ovate, 2.5-10cm (2-4in) long, alternate, aromatic
Flower small, many yellow stamens, in axillary clusters, March-May
Fruit purple-black berry

USES

Culinary leaves used, fresh or dried, for many savoury dishes, especially meat, in marinades for flavouring and tenderizing, in stock, rice dishes, with blandly flavoured vegetables; half a leaf is sufficient for one dish
Medicinal leaves, berries and oil; for flatulence; burning leaves antiseptic; oil for sprains and bruises
Cosmetic none
Domestic for strewing and as a general household insecticide; wood used for marquetry
Fragrance and Aroma whole plant strongly aromatic, and wood sweet-scented; leaves used in potpourri

RECIPE

Soused herrings
2 herrings
1 bayleaf
150ml/¼ pint/⅔ cup cider vinegar
150ml/¼ pint/⅔ cup water
salt and pepper
Clean the fish and remove any roes and the backbone from each. Season each half with salt and freshly-ground black pepper, put a quarter of a bay leaf on each and roll up tightly. Pack into a shallow oven-proof dish, and cover with vinegar and water. Cover with kitchen foil. Bake at 350°F/180°C/Gas Mark 4 for ¾-1 hour. Serve cold with the remaining liquid. Serve with wedges of lemon and thin brown bread and butter.

bay leaves

dried bay leaves

soused herrings

Bergamot

American herbs such as this one have a history associated with the original Indian inhabitants of the North American continent including Canada, and it was Oswego Indians in particular who used the leaves as the beverage which gives it one of its common names. Flavour is reminiscent of fragrant China tea, making it a most acceptable afternoon drink, but it also has some medicinal use. The whole plant smells pleasantly of the bergamot orange, *Citrus bergamia*, from Spain, whose essential oil is part of the recipe for Eau de Cologne. Bergamot is a highly decorative garden plant, and a favourite with bees; besides the species, there are varieties with rose-pink, purple, or salmon-pink flowers.

Cultivation A handsome perennial for the herbaceous border, bergamot can be planted in autumn or spring, preferably in sun and a well-drained but moist soil – a sandy one with plenty of rotted organic matter added just before planting and in spring annually is ideal. Allow 45cm (18in) between plants, and expect them to be slow to establish. 'Croftway Pink' and 'Cambridge Scarlet' are two good varieties. Increase is by division in spring, and seed sown at the same time can be used for the species. Bergamot is a good cut flower, and will supply stems all summer.

USES

Culinary fresh or dried leaves for tea; fresh leaves in salads, and as garnishes; sparingly in cheeses
Medicinal leaves as a tea to relieve stomach troubles, also for inhaling the vapour to relieve bronchial congestion and catarrh
Cosmetic once used in hair preparations, now in sun-tan oils and creams
Domestic for perfuming candles
Fragrance and Aroma whole plant, particularly leaves; used in pot-pourris; essential oil for perfumery

RECIPE

Bergamot tea (for nausea and vomiting)
In the US, bergamot was immortalized as the substitute for Indian tea by those colonists who supported the famous Boston Tea Party.
To make the tea, pour 600ml/1 pint/2½ cups of boiling water over 25g/1oz/¾ cup bergamot leaves. This herb tea is mildly relaxing and soporific, and relieves symptoms of nausea and vomiting.

Bergamot vapour
Bergamot leaves also make an effective vapour treatment for the relief of bronchial catarrh and throat infections due to their high thymol content; to prepare, pour boiling water onto a large handful of leaves in a bowl and inhale the vapour.

IDENTIFICATION

Height 60-105cm (2-3½ft), spread 30-38cm (12-15in)
Root fibrous, forming a thick mat
Stem square, tough and hard
Leaf toothed, ovate-lanceolate, hairy, dark green, sometimes tinged red, 5-15cm, (2-6in) long, opposite
Flower red, tubular, two-lipped, up to 5cm (2in) long, in shaggy clusters at the tops of stems, June-September
Seed black
Leaves the most aromatic part of the plant; even the roots give off fragrance

bergamot flowers

bergamot leaves

bergamot tea

Borage

Its chief virtue lies in its medicinal qualities which were once thought considerable; even now it has some use in the treatment of ailments. Borage has star-shaped flowers of an intense blue rarely seen in other plants and these, together with its long-flowering tendency, ease of cultivation, and hardiness, make it one of the best garden plants. Popular with bees, it is native of Europe including Britain and grows in temperate and warm regions in North America.

Pliny named the plant Euphrosinum because it was thought to bring happiness and joy, and the Greeks and Romans both regarded it as not only a comforting plant, but also as a supplier of courage. This belief persisted down the centuries so that by Gerard's time, he was still able to quote the tag: *'Ego Borage gaudia semper ago'* (I, Borage, bring always courage). It was even said to be the Nepenthe described by Homer which, when taken with wine, brought absolute forgetfulness.

Cultivation Cultivation is easy; sow the seeds thinly outdoors in spring, preferably in a sandy soil and a sunny position; it will, however, grow in shade and moist soil. Allow 23-30cm (9-12in) between plants. It will self-sow during the season, and such plants may still be flowering in November in mild autumns and sheltered gardens.

IDENTIFICATION

Height 45cm (18in), spread 30cm (12in)
Root fibrous, shallow
Stem hairy, hollow, succulent, branching
Leaf oval, pointed, alternate, roughly hairy, to 10cm (4in) long and 3.5cm (1½in) wide
Flower five intensely blue, star-shaped petals, prominent purple stamen column, flower to 2.5cm (1in) wide, in drooping clusters, April-October.
Seed black

USES

Culinary cucumber-flavoured juicy leaves in fruit cups, summer punches, fruit drinks, salads, garnishes; candied flowers for confectionary and cake decoration; can be used as spinach substitute, is rich in calcium and potassium
Medicinal leaves for poultices, diuretic; an infusion of the leaves for coughs; the whole plant contains mucilage which gives it its demulcent quality
Cosmetic leaf preparations for softening and cleaning the skin
Domestic none
Fragrance and Aroma none

PRESCRIPTION

Borage syrup (for kidney and bladder inflammations)
Purée 200g/½lb of fresh flowering plant in a blender. Strain through muslin cloth and make into a cordial syrup with 200g/½lb/1 cup white sugar. One tablespoon per day is taken for treatment of kidney and bladder inflammations.
Borage tea (for reduction of temperature)
Historically, all parts of this herb – the leaves, flowers and seeds – were prized for their ability to 'expel pensiveness and melancholy; an action not explained by modern research which reveals non-specific anti-inflammatory and mildly diuretic properties. Its high calcium and potassium salts contents assist in the reduction of temperatures when taken as a hot tea (simmer for 5 minutes, small handful of fresh leaves with 600ml/1 pint/2½ cups of boiling water). The fresh leaves used in a summer salad will increase the flow of milk in nursing mothers.

borage seeds

dried borage leaves

borage syrup

borage leaves

Burnet, Salad

There are two burnets grown for herbal use: great burnet, *Sanguisorba officinalis*, and this one, formerly called *S. minor*, or lesser burnet. Both have the same medicinal properties, but salad burnet has been much used in salads, from the days of the Elizabethans.

Salad burnet is a European plant, native to Britain where it grows on chalky soil amongst grass, such as the downlands of the south. It can be grown in all parts of the United States. The graceful ferny leaves make it an attractive, low-growing plant for edgings to borders in herb-gardens or beds in mixed plantings; it is virtually evergreen. The cucumber flavour of the leaves is similar to borage, but with a slightly nutty overtone.

Cultivation As salad burnet is a wild European plant it is easily grown there, or in any temperate climate where the soil is chalky and well-drained. A sheltered sunny position suits it best, and it can be sown or planted outdoors in spring, and spaced 15-23cm (6-9in) apart. Remove the flowerheads for better leaf production unless seed is wanted. However, it can also be easily increased by division in autumn. The leaves will linger well into the winter, and sprout very early in spring.

USES

Culinary fresh leaves in salads, sauces, summer wine punches, fruit cups, soups added as a garnish at the last minute

Medicinal fresh leaf, whole plant fresh or dried, dried root; fresh leaves help digestion; decoction of the roots to stop bleeding

Cosmetic use infusion of the leaves for cooling sunburn

Domestic none

Fragrance and aroma none

PRESCRIPTION

Burnet compress (for the relief of sunburn)

1 handful of salad burnet leaves
600ml/1 pint/2½ cups boiling water
Slightly bruise the leaves, add the boiling water, cover the bowl and allow to stand for about 10 minutes. Strain and cool. To use, soak gauze dressing in the infusion and apply to the affected part as often as required until relief is felt.

ROSACEAE *Poterium sanguisorba*
Herbaceous perennial

IDENTIFICATION

Height flowering stems to 20-40cm (10-20in), spread 23cm (9in)

Root fibrous, spreading, dark brown to black

Stem smooth, slender, slightly branched

Leaf blue-green, fern-like, up to 15cm (6in) long, with 7-11 rounded, toothed leaflets in pairs

Flower reddish to green, small, in a ball-like head 1.5cm (½in) wide at the end of a stem, early-late summer

Seed tiny, inconspicuous

salad burnet seeds

salad burnet

burnet compress

Caraway

Caraway seed cake was one of the staples of the Victorian teatable; you either adored or hated the taste of the little black seeds. Nowadays caraway has a much more extensive use in cooking, being mixed with savoury as well as sweet dishes, and the strong and distinctive flavour can almost be considered a spice. The plant is not particularly decorative; it is native of southern Europe, and Asia to India and grows in temperate to warm regions in North America.

Caraway is one of the most ancient of herbs, and it was valued by the Arabs and Egyptians of 5,000 years ago, who called it *Karawya*. It is still an everyday ingredient of Middle Eastern cookery, and also finds favour in Continental dishes. It is frequently added to sauerkraut and Kummel, the German liqueur, contains its oil, along with cumin; in Britain, during the Middle Ages and Tudor times, baked fruit was flavoured with the ubiquitous seeds.

Cultivation Easily grown, caraway should be sown outdoors in early autumn when ripe, in sun or a little shade, and any reasonable soil. Thin to about 20cm (8in), and keep free of weeds. Harvest the seeds in July-August by cutting the seedheads just before the first seeds start to fall, and hanging them over a tray in a dry airy place.

IDENTIFICATION

Height 45-60cm (18-24in), spread 30cm (12in)
Root thick, tapering, pale, parsnip-like but smaller
Stem slender, hollow, ribbed, branching, erect, appearing in 2nd year
Leaves feathery, light green, carrot-like
Flower white to pinkish, tiny, in umbel-like clusters, June-July
Seed actually the fruits, black, ridged, aromatic and strongly flavoured

USES

Culinary seeds in bread, cheeses, stewed fruits, cakes, biscuits, with pork, goulash and other fatty meats, fresh leaves in salads, soups and with mild cheeses, roots boiled as vegetable
Medicinal fresh leaves, roots, seeds have digestive properties
Cosmetic none
Domestic none
Fragrance and Aroma seeds and leaves when bruised

RECIPE

Cheese and caraway potatoes
4 large potatoes
100g/4oz/1 cup grated gruyère cheese
salt and pepper to taste
Scrub but do not peel the potatoes and cut them in half lengthwise. Wrap in a boat of greased foil and sprinkle each half with some grated cheese and a little caraway. Preheat the oven to 180°C/350°F/Gas Mark 4 and cook for 30-45 minutes or until the potatoes are soft.

caraway seeds

caraway leaves

cheese and
caraway potatoes

Catmint

OTHER NAMES: Catnip

LABIATAE *Nepeta cataria*
Herbaceous perennial

The blue-flowered garden species of this genus (*N.* x *faassenii*), also called catmint, is highly decorative, with its grey leaves and long-lasting flower spikes, but *N. cataria* is the true herb, of little known but considerable medical use, for which it has a long history, back to Gerard's day and earlier, though it is not so used nowadays. There is good reason for its common name; the bruised foliage, whose odour has mint-like associations, induces cats to roll all over the plant, eventually ruining it, but it is said that plants grown from seed will be safe until dying down, or withering for some reason. Plants grown from divisions or cuttings have little chance of survival after planting, unless rigorously defended from the local feline population. Catmint is native to Asia, Europe including Britain, mainly the south, and is grown in cool, temperate regions in North America.

Cultivation Seed can be sown in late summer or spring, in dryish soil tending to alkaline, though it must be potentially fertile, and sun or a little shade; division in spring is also possible. Distance apart is about 40cm (20in). The grey leaves and white flowers combine to produce a pretty, easily grown border plant, beloved by bees. The garden hybrid *N.* x *faassenii*, has long spikes of light lavender-coloured flowers, with a second flowering in autumn, if the faded spikes are removed immediately after flowering.

IDENTIFICATION

Height 45-90cm (2-3ft), spread 40cm (20in); whole plant is downy
Root fibrous, spreading
Stem square, erect, branching
Leaf grey-green, heart-shaped, coarsely toothed, up to 7.5cm (3in) long, opposite
Flower 2-lipped-tubular, white, sometimes pale blue, purple-dotted, small, 6mm (¼in) long, in clusters at end of stems, June-September
Seed brown, viable for five years

USES

Culinary fresh leaves in moderation to flavour sauce
Medicinal flowering tops fresh or dried for colds, catarrh, bronchitis; as a soothing drink for sleeplessness, stress and irritability
Cosmetic for hair care, helps it to grow
Domestic repellent for rats
Fragrance and Aroma strongly aromatic when bruised, considered unpleasantly so by some people

HOUSEHOLD USE

Stuffing for toy mice
Dry the leaves first, and break them up into small pieces. Stuff toy mice made out of rabbit fur, for kittens and for elderly cats in need of exercise. Use as a strewing herb if rats are suspected anywhere, grow in the garden for a similar reason, and put bunches into hen and duck houses to discourage rats from there also.

catmint toy mouse

dried catmint leaves

catmint leaves

ground catmint leaves

COMPOSITAE
Chamaemelum nobile, syn.
Anthemis nobilis
Perennial

IDENTIFICATION

Height mat-like, flowering stems 30cm (12in)
Root fibrous, shallow
Stem hairy, branching, green
Leaf grey-green, finely-divided into many thread-like segments, giving the whole plant a feathery appearance
Flower daisy-like, to 3cm (1¼in) wide, white outer petals, yellow conical centre, July-September
Seed light brown, oblong

ground chamomile flowerheads

Chamomile

OTHER NAMES: Camomile

The true or Roman chamomile is pleasantly aromatic, with a distinct odour of apples, and this explains its common name – it is derived from the Greeks who named it 'ground-apple' from *kamai*, on the ground, and *melon*, apple. The name of the Spanish sherry Manzinilla means 'little apple', and it is flavoured with this plant.

Low-growing, almost mat-like, with white daisy flowers in summer, chamomile dates back to at least the time of the ancient Egyptians who are said to have used it for curing ague. It is illustrated in an English manuscript of the 13th century, was used in the time of Gerard, and later by Culpeper, and altogether was so well-known and commonly used medicinally, that it was thought 'but lost time and labour to describe it'. It is a native of southern Europe and grows in temperate to warm regions in North America.

The wild chamomile, which is sometimes confused with it, is *Matricaria recutita*, or scented mayweed, an annual native to Europe including Britain.

Both chamomiles are cultivated mainly for their medicinal properties, and Roman chamomile has a further use as a grass substitute for lawns.

Cultivation The double-flowered form is the one generally cultivated because it is preferred for medical use, and is grown from division of runners, taken and planted in early spring; seedlings produce a large number of single-flowered forms. Fertile, moist soil and sun are necessary, and spacing should be 23cm (9in) each way, unless it is to be used for lawns, when spacing should be 15cm (6in). For such use, the non-flowering variety 'Treneague' is to be preferred, and can be grown in a little shade. Young plants should be kept free of weeds. Chamomile makes a good lawn, provided it does not have too much traffic on it, but should be used for small areas, as it needs constant attention to keep weeds at bay, but it will have the advantage of remaining green in dry conditions.

USES

Culinary none
Medicinal dried flowers as tisane for flatulence, dyspepsia and other stomach troubles; as a mild sedative; powerful antiseptic; tonic for poor appetite
Cosmetic dried flowers for lightening blonde hair; skin cleanser; softening rough skin
Domestic as a dye, orange or green-brown (*Anthemis tinctoria*, dyer's chamomile), to prevent fungus diseases on plants, activator for compost heaps
Fragrance and Aroma whole plant apple-scented

PRESCRIPTION

Chamomile tea
Chamomile's highly scented dried flowerheads contain up to one per cent of an aromatic oil which possesses powerfully antiseptic and anti-inflammatory properties of the herb. Taken as a tea (25g/1oz/¾ cup to 600ml/1pint/2½ cups boiling water) it promotes gastric secretions and improves the appetite, while an infusion of the same strength can be used as an internal antiseptic douche, a gargle for mouth ulcers, or an external compress for skin rashes or allergies.
Chamomile oil (for allergic skin rashes)
A chamomile oil can be made by tightly packing the flowerheads into a preserving jar, covering with olive oil, and leaving in the sun for 3 weeks. After decanting, the oil can be employed in skin preparations by those prone to allergic rashes.

chamomile leaves

dried chamomile flowers

chamomile oil

chamomile tea

Chervil

Chervil is an easily grown herb which has a short life-cycle of one season. Although a native of such areas as the Middle East and the Caucasus, it is largely used only in French cooking. This is a pity as its delicate, lacy leaves have an unusual flavour, which helps to lift recipes out of the everyday routine.

Almost certainly brought to Britain by the Romans, it is now occasionally found growing wild, and can easily be confused with cow parsley when the latter is young. However, cow parsley is perennial and eventually grows much taller and stouter, with large leaves lacking the sweet distinctive aroma of chervil.

Cultivation Chervil grows quickly, provided it has moist soil and a slightly shady place. It does not like a hot dry position and in such a place, seeds will not germinate until heavy rain occurs. Basically, chervil requires moist, cloudy weather, so that a typical English summer suits it well.

Sow the seed in early to mid-spring, or late summer, preferably the latter as viability falls rapidly, outdoors where they are to grow – chervil does not do well if transplanted. Thin the seedlings to 23cm (9in) apart, and thereafter keep free of weeds, and water well in dry weather.

Leaves can be collected from six weeks after germination, and thereafter continuously, provided the flowering stems are removed. The late summer sowings will provide leaves through the winter, as it very hardy.

It does well in a container, preferably a window-box, in which it is the only herb, sowing half in spring and half in late summer to provide a succession of leaves.

USES

Culinary chopped leaves best added fresh, in large quantities just before serving, as the light flavour is quickly lost; add to soups, particularly sorrel or spinach; all egg dishes; salads; Bechamel sauce; ingredient in *fines herbes*; sprinkle over roast meats, or make herb butter to rub over poultry

Medicinal little use; fresh leaf may be applied to aching joints in a warm poultice

Cosmetic fresh leaves can be infused to make a skin cleanser

Domestic virtually no use

Fragrance and Aroma leaves aromatic, mixture of aniseed and liquorice, fleeting after cutting; root similar aroma

RECIPE

Glazed baby carrots with chervil
1kg/2lbs young carrots
50g/2oz/¼ cup butter
1 teaspoon sugar
1 tbls chopped chervil
salt and ground pepper to taste
Remove the green tops from the carrots and scrape them. Put them in a saucepan of salted boiling water and cook for about 8 minutes (they should still be slightly firm). Drain and set aside. In a clean saucepan, melt the butter and sugar over a gentle heat. Add the carrots and turn them frequently to coat them with the pale glaze. Cook gently for a further 10 minutes, turning the carrots all the time. Add the salt and pepper and sprinkle with the chervil.

UMBELLIFERAE *Anthriscus cerefolium*
Hardy annual

IDENTIFICATION

Height 45-50cm (18-20in), spread 20cm (8in)

Root tap-root, white and tapering, aromatic

Leaf 3-pinnate, each leaflet twice-divided, lacy, delicate, light green, each leaf up to 10cm (4in) long, becoming reddish with age, leaf-stems sheath the main stem

Stem hollow, ridged, upright, slightly hairy

Flower white, tiny, flat-topped clusters forming an umbel, mid-late summer

Seed long, thin, biscuit-coloured

chervil seeds

chervil leaves

glazed carrots with chervil

Chives

Chives are amongst the most well-known of culinary herbs, and their delicate onion flavour has been added to food where the stronger onion would overwhelm everything else, for hundreds of years. The grass-like leaves grow in clumps, and can be picked outdoors fresh from February to November, longer if given protection. Although rarely found in the wild now, this native of Europe including Britain, was sometimes also known in the Middle Ages as 'rush-leek' from the Greek *schoinos*, rush and *prason*, leek. It thrives in temperate and warm to hot regions of North America.

Cultivation Chives need a light, but moist well-drained soil and sun, or a little shade. Clumps can be divided and replanted in mid-spring, about 15cm (6in) apart, or seed sown in April or late August, and thinned. Removal of the flower-stems before flowering increases leaf production, but the flowers are pretty, and leaves are always present, even if fewer. The plants provide surprisingly ornamental edgings to beds and borders, and also grow well in pots which enable them to be protected, and thereby extend the season both early and late.

IDENTIFICATION

Height 15-30cm (6-9in), clumps about 15cm (6in) wide; variety *sibiricum* to 38cm (15in) tall.
Root white, narrow-bulbous
Stem erect, smooth, grey-green
Leaf hollow, round, grey-green, rush-like
Flower tiny, lilac-purple, in clusters forming a roundish head like a pincushion, July-August, long-lasting; *A.s. sibiricum* has rose coloured flowers
Seed black

USES

Culinary fresh leaves, chopped, in salads, sandwiches, sprinkled on soups, savoury toasts, omelettes and other egg dishes, with cheeses
Medicinal little, but leaves are mildly antiseptic, have some tonic effect and can relieve rheumatism
Cosmetic none
Domestic said to prevent scab infection on apples
Fragrance and Aroma aromatic of onions

RECIPE

Chive butter
Can be used in scrambled eggs and omelettes, on cooked vegetables and with grilled lamb, beef or fish
100g/4oz/¹/₂ cup butter
4 tbls chopped chives
1 tbls lemon juice
salt and pepper
Cream the chives and softened butter together until they are well mixed. Beat in the lemon juice and add salt and pepper to taste. Cover and cool the butter in the refrigerator until ready to use. It will keep for several days in the refrigerator.

chive seeds

chive butter

chopped chives

chive leaves

scrambled eggs with chive butter

Clary

The genus *Salvia* is a large one, containing a variety of plant types and including species from temperate and subtropical parts of the world. Sage is one of the species, and there are blue and red-flowered varieties of salvia which are grown purely for garden ornament. Clary was once thought to have great medicinal value, especially for the eyes – clary is a derivation of clear-eye – but now is mainly grown for decoration. The clary listed in seed catalogues is *S. horminum*, an annual with large bracts, petal-like, purple, rose-pink, white or blue.

In the 16th century it was used in the brewing of beer and ale, which resulted in their being more potent. William Turner, a botanist of the time remarked that 'it restores natural heat, and comforts the vital spirits, and helps the memory, and quickens the senses'. Clary leaves were used to make fritters, mixing lemon-peel, nutmeg and brandy into the batter!

Cultivation Clary is easily grown from seed sown in spring, and thinned to about 23cm (9in) apart each way. Most soils and sites will suit it, and it should be kept free of weeds while establishing. Flowering stems will be produced in the second year, and thereafter it will self-sow. The leaves are at their best in spring.

USES

Culinary fresh leaves used in fritters, home-made wine and beer, omelettes, soup, salads
Medicinal seed to make eye lotion; infused leaves as gargle, antiseptic skin wash, and to treat vomiting
Cosmetic not generally used
Domestic not generally used
Fragrance and Aroma strongly aromatic reminiscent of balsam, slightly bitter-tasting; essential oil (clary oil, muscatel sage), used as a perfume fixative, for which it is mainly commercially grown nowadays

PRESCRIPTION

Clary eye lotion (to remove grit from the eyes)
Soak about 6 clary seeds in clean warm water, previously boiled. Leave the seeds to swell until they are mucilaginous. Then carefully introduce these into the corner of the eye on a cotton bud. Particles of grit will adhere to the mucilage and make grit easy to remove.
Clary compress (for boils)
Steep 50g/2oz of dried clary leaves in 600ml/1 pint/2½ cups of vinegar for 2 weeks. Apply as a compress for the treatment of boils.

IDENTIFICATION

Height 60-90cm (2-3ft), spread 30-38cm (12-15in)
Root fibrous, shallow, little-spreading
Stem square, light green to brown, downy
Leaf downy beneath, oblong, much wrinkled, toothed, 15-23cm (6-9in) long, dull green
Flower two-lipped tubular, white and lilac or pink, 1.5-2cm (½-¾in) long, in downy leafy spikes June-October; bracts large, purple or pink
Seed dark brown to black especially in sun
The plant is strongly aromatic, the garden clary barely so

clary seeds

dried clary

clary compress

clary leaves

clary eye lotion

Comfrey

IDENTIFICATION

Height 90-120cm (3-4ft), spread 60cm (2ft)
Root outside black, flesh white, juicy, deeply penetrating, to at least 120cm (4ft), thick and tapering, also fibrous
Stem bristly-hairy, hollow, stout, branching, angled
Leaf hairy, green; lower, 25cm (10in) long, broad-lanceolate, upper not as large, narrower, and running down the stem
Flower in drooping, one-sided, downy clusters, flowers bell-shaped, creamy yellow or purple, May-September
Seed black

Comfrey is one of the herbs that seem to have been a remedy for all ills, and one that the mediaeval and Elizabethan physicians and herbalists would never be without. Its common name points to its apparently miraculous healing powers and, though it does not literally cause the ends of broken bones to weld together again, it will certainly hold them securely together and in contact, if the pounded root is bound round a break – the mixture will set when dry. Moreover, the roots or leaves used as fomentations are of considerable use when applied to sprains, swellings, and bruises, and as a poultice to cuts, boils and abscesses.

Comfrey is a native of Europe including Britain, and Asia, preferring damp situations. It also grows in temperate to warm regions of North America. *S.* x *uplandicum* is the Russian comfrey, a hybrid between *S. officinale* and *S. asperum*, with rose-pink to blue flowers, and the garden variety of this, Bocking No. 14, is the most useful for garden plants, as it is a good mulch and supplier of liquid plant food and contains a high proportion of potash. It contains considerable protein also, about 35 per cent, but only for animal consumption.

Cultivation Comfrey should be grown from divisions taken in spring or autumn or from pieces of root with a bud attached. Spacing is 60cm (2ft) each way, and sun or shade are acceptable. Soil should be deep and moist. Site should be chosen carefully, as it is difficult to get all the deeply penetrating root out, should this be necessary, and any left will produce fresh plants. Comfrey will live at least 20 years, and is decorative enough to grow in the garden, as well as being extremely useful in plant nutrition.

RECIPE

Comfrey cleansing oil (for dry skins)
As well as cleansing the skin, comfrey oil also reduces puffiness, and softens and conditions the skin. Add as many comfrey leaves as possible to 300ml/½ pint/1¼ cups of almond oil in a jar. Seal the jar and leave to steep in a warm place for 2-3 weeks, shaking the jar regularly. Finally, strain the oil discarding the leaves and apply to the face on cotton wool pads.

USES

Culinary young leaves as alternative to spinach; blanched stems once used like celery
Medicinal considerable, as described left
Cosmetic leaves and roots for healing and soothing in skin care
Domestic as dye, use fresh leaves, stalks and flowers to provide yellow or orange depending on mordant
Fragrance and Aroma none

comfrey oil

dried comfrey leaves

creeping comfrey

comfrey leaves

dried comfrey root

Coriander

A culinary herb, whose seed and leaves are the main parts used, coriander is one of the ingredients of curry powder and hence found in many Indian recipes. The seeds are distinctively spicy, profusely produced by the plant, and combine well with cumin and other spices to produce the flavours in much Middle-Eastern and South-east Asian food; curiously, when fresh the seeds smell of bed-bugs, but as they mature, smell very pleasantly of oranges.

Coriander is indigenous to southern Europe and is naturalized in southern Britain, but it is a widely-used herb, being part of the cooking of Egypt, India, North Africa, North America, Peru (along with chillis), China and Northern Europe. It was much used in mediaeval times in Britain and, indeed, its use can be traced back for 3,000 years.

Cultivation Coriander seed is sown outdoors in sun and a light, well-drained soil in April-May, and thinned to about 20cm (8in) apart. It grows quickly to about 60cm (2ft) tall, flowers profusely, and sets seed without any difficulty. Watch the seed carefully, as it ripens suddenly and will fall without warning; alternatively cut the flower stems just as the smell of the seeds starts to change and become pleasant, and hang to finish ripening in paper bags.

USES

Culinary seeds for flavouring a variety of dishes where spicy flavour is required, used whole or as a freshly-made powder; fresh leaves used in the same way, especially with Indian recipes, with salads, marinades, rice, and with bread
Medicinal as digestive for colic, griping and flatulence
Cosmetic not generally used
Domestic not generally used
Fragrance and Aroma strongly and unpleasantly aromatic, seeds used in potpourris

RECIPE

Thai coriander and garlic marinade
This marinade adds an exotic flavour to pork chops or steak. A whole piece of loin of pork or beef fillet can be seasoned in the same way and roasted in the oven.
400g/1lb pork chops or fillet steak
1 tbls ground coriander seeds
¼ tablespoon ground black pepper
4 cloves of garlic
1 tbls Thai fish sauce
1½ tbls light soy sauce
Pound the garlic, coriander seeds and black pepper in a mortar so that they form a paste. Add the soy and fish sauce (if fish sauce is not available, use another tablespoon of soy sauce) and mix well. Spoon over the meat and leave to marinate for at least two hours, preferably overnight. Grill or roast the meat in the usual way, basting it with the marinade.

UMBELLIFERAE
Coriandrum sativum
Hardy annual

IDENTIFICATION

Height 45-60cm (18-24in), spread about 20cm (8in)
Root in shape like a long thin carrot, with a few fibrous roots, pale brown
Stem erect, green branching, smooth, thin
Leaf bright green; lower ones pinnate and shiny, broadly lobed, upper thread-like and feathery
Flower tiny, white to pale lilac, in umbel clusters, July-September
Seed ball-like, light brown, strongly aromatic
Whole plant strongly and unpleasantly aromatic

Thai coriander & garlic marinade

ground coriander seeds

coriander seeds

chopped coriander leaves

COMPOSITAE
Chrysanthemum balsamita
Herbaceous perennial

IDENTIFICATION

Height flowering stems 90cm (3ft), spread 75cm (2½ft)
Root creeping, somewhat fibrous, rapidly spreading
Stem erect, smooth, green, tough
Leaf grey-green, up to 27cm (11in) long, oblong, barely roundly-serrated, two small lobes at base of some leaves
Flower yellow, small, in loose clusters on top of stem, late summer, do not seed in Britain, not produced if plant in shade

Costmary

OTHER NAMES: Alecost

Only a hundred years ago, costmary could be found in almost any cottage garden, in fact in most gardens throughout Britain. Now it is rarely seen, though the present herb revival is ensuring that it is once more being propagated and distributed. It had considerable domestic use, and its alternative common name gives the clue to its culinary use. A native of southern Europe and western Asia, costmary is now naturalized in Europe and North America, being introduced in Britain at least as early as the beginning of the 15th century when it was detailed as an ingredient in cookery books of the time. Culpeper wrote of it 'it is so frequently known to be an inhabitant in almost every garden that it is needless to write a description thereof'. In Colonial times in North America, the leaf was often used as a bookmark in bibles and prayerbooks and so acquired the nickname 'Bible leaf.' It grows into a tall plant, with a large rosette of basal leaves, and is pleasantly aromatic, with a balsam-like odour.

Cultivation Allow plenty of space for costmary as its roots spread widely, and it will grow at least 90cm (3ft) tall. Sun is necessary for flowers, and most soils will suit; it does well in dry conditions. Plant in spring or autumn from divisions, 60cm (2ft) apart; the stems will probably need some support.

USES

Culinary once used in preparation of beer and ale in place of hops; can be used now in salads, sauces and soups, but in small quantities
Medicinal not so used
Cosmetic use infused leaves in water for washing or bathing, and for hairwashing
Domestic as insect repellent, use dried leaves, alone or mixed with other herbs
Fragrance and Aroma leaves strongly aromatic, used dried in potpourri

HOUSEHOLD USE

Costmary rinsing water (to perfume household linen)
100g/4oz fresh costmary leaves (or 2 tbls dried)
600ml/1 pint/2½ cups boiling water
Put the costmary leaves in a bowl, add the boiling water, cover and leave to infuse for at least 2 hours. Strain and add to the rinsing water when laundering sheets and other household linen.

costmary rinsing water

costmary leaves

Cotton Lavender

OTHER NAMES: Lavender cotton

A strongly aromatic, somewhat bitter-tasting plant, cotton lavender is not a lavender at all, but a member of the daisy family. Its main use was in medicine, but it also had some domestic application, and was a regular part of mediaeval life in Britain. The southern Mediterranean region is its home, and it was used for many centuries by the Arabs. It grows well in warm to hot regions of North America. Cotton lavender is a decorative garden plant for the silver or grey border and traditionally was one of the plants chosen for edging the geometrical beds of the Elizabethan knot gardens.

Cultivation Cotton lavender needs a dry sunny situation in light soil to ensure that it ripens fully and is thus better able to withstand cold. Moist heavy soil is not suitable, and likely to cause its death, especially in severe cold. Plant in late spring, and clip in mid-spring if required to be grown formally as edging, or to keep it within the space available. Remove flowering stems to maintain dense leafy growth. Increase is from short, semi-hardwood cuttings with a heel, early to midsummer, put into a sandy compost and covered.

USES

Culinary none
Medicinal occasionally as a vermifuge, its traditional use
Cosmetic none
Domestic to repel household insects, as a strewing herb beneath carpets, and in linen and clothing
Fragrance and Aroma leaves and stems strongly aromatic; oil for perfumery is extracted from it

HOUSEHOLD USE

Cotton lavender sweetbag (against moths)
Use crushed cotton lavender leaves, dried, as part of a mixture to prevent moths invading clothes and linen. Mix them with: equal parts crushed dried rosemary leaves and rue, together with ½ part powdered cloves *or* 1 part dried lavender flower spikes. Make up into sachets with ribbon to hang amongst clothes or slip between blankets, sheets and so on.

IDENTIFICATION

Height 45-60cm (18-24in), spread similar
Root fibrous, compact, one or two anchoring roots
Stem woody, brown, grey-felted, much branched from base
Leaf silver-grey-green, evergreen, 2.5-4cm (1-1½in) long, closely packed, 3mm (⅛in) wide, margins deeply indented
Flower yellow, rounded, so freely borne as to appear in clusters, on stems 15cm (6in) long, July-August
Seed brown, with a pappus

ground cotton lavender leaves

cotton lavender sweetbag ingredients

dried cotton lavender leaves

Dandelion

If the dandelion was a rare plant, it would be thought a highly desirable garden species, since the flowers are large and brilliantly yellow. But it is depressingly abandoned in its ability to increase, and difficult to uproot, so finds no favour with gardeners. However, it has considerable medicinal applications, and various culinary uses which are becoming more and more popular.

Dandelions are natives of Europe and Asia, and botanically they form a difficult and much varied group with many microspecies, but for the herbalist's purposes, these are of no moment. Its common name is derived from the French *dent de lion*, lion's-tooth, possibly from the shape of the leaves of the plant. In Culpeper's time, it was apparently 'vulgarly called Piss-a-beds', a reference no doubt to its diuretic qualities, and preserved in its French name *pissenlit*.

Cultivation Details on how to grow dandelions are generally superfluous; the real need is usually to know how to eradicate them. The root is least tenacious in early spring and easiest to dig up complete, and if removed at this time, will prevent the further problem of spreading by seed later in the season. Sections of the root can be used for increase, and any piece of the taproot left behind will sprout again.

IDENTIFICATION

Height flowering stem to 15-23cm (6-9in), spread of leaves similar
Root tap-rooted, brown-black on the outside, white inside, tough, tenacious, tapering from 2-3cm (1-1¼in) wide, at least 15cm (6in) long
Stem hollow, rounded, light green-yellow, producing milky juice, unbranched
Leaf in a basal rosette, oblong to spatulate, shiny, edges much cut into large jagged serrations, sometimes themselves also serrated, between 7.5 and 15cm (3 and 6in) long
Flower solitary, brilliant yellow, 3.5-5cm (1½-2in) wide, made up of many tightly packed strap-shaped florets, April-November
Seed pale brown, each with a pappus forming the dandelion 'clock' of a fluffy ball

USES

Culinary root dried, roasted and ground as coffee substitute; young leaves in salads, sandwiches, or chopped up for mixing with soups and vegetables; blanching the leaves will result in a sweeter flavour; leaves and flowers to make wine; the leaves for dandelion stout
Medicinal all parts of considerable use in liver troubles, a good diuretic and tonic, also mild laxative; juice said to be effective in treating warts
Cosmetic not for general use
Domestic a dye from the root, magenta with alum, yellow to brown with iron; domestic rabbits can be fed with fresh leaves
Fragrance and Aroma somewhat unpleasantly bitter aroma when injured

RECIPE

Dandelion and bacon salad
225g/8oz/½lb young dandelion leaves
100g/4oz/¼lb streaky bacon diced
1cm/½in slice of white bread, cubed
4 tablespoons olive or walnut oil
1 tbls white wine vinegar
1 clove garlic, crushed
salt and freshly ground pepper
oil for cooking
Wash and dry the leaves and tear them into a salad bowl. Make a vinaigrette using olive oil and vinegar, and season to taste, adding a little sugar if desired. Fry the bacon, crushed garlic and bread in oil until golden-brown. Pour the contents of the pan over the leaves and turn the leaves so they are thoroughly coated. Add the vinaigrette, toss again and serve soon after making.

dandelion leaves

dried dandelion leaves

dried dandelion root

dandelion & bacon salad

Dill

Although this herb has its origin in southern Europe and western Asia, its common name is said to derive either from the Anglo-Saxon *dylle* or the old Norse *dilla* which meant to soothe or lull, in reference to its use in calming infants who had hiccups – in fact Culpeper said 'it stayeth the hiccough.'

Dill-water or gripe-water is, at any rate, several hundred years old in usage, and is still called upon today.

It was found amongst the names of herbs used by Egyptian doctors 5,000 years ago and remains of the plant have been found in the ruins of Roman buildings in Britain. Use was widespread in northern Europe in the Middle Ages, and the seeds and leaves are especially popular today in Norwegian and Swedish recipes. The feathery leaves and bright yellow flowers are worth growing for their decorativeness alone and, being an annual, they soon pay for their place.

Cultivation Dill is grown from the flat oval seeds sown outdoors from April-early June, in well-drained, poor soil and full sun. It should be sown where it is to grow, as it transplants badly, and thinned to 23cm (9in) each way. If grown close to fennel, they will cross-pollinate freely, and the resultant seeds will be hybrids between the two. In good hot summers, dill will grow rampantly and strongly, but may need support if there is much wind. Self-sowing is likely; seeds should be collected on their stems just before they are ripe enough to drop, and placed in paper bags hung in a warm dry airy place. Watch for greenfly in crowded conditions.

USES

Culinary fresh leaves, chopped and used for garnish, and sauces, in fish dishes, yoghurt, cream; seeds for vinegars, with pickles, cucumbers, cakes and pastry
Medicinal oil of dill to make dill water for infantile flatulence; seeds have sedative effect and stave off hunger
Cosmetic none
Domestic none
Fragrance and Aroma reminiscent of caraway, with an additional odour, whole plant, particularly the seeds, used in perfumery

RECIPE

Pickled salmon
This traditional Scandinavian dish, known as *gravad lax*, can be made with either fresh or frozen salmon.
420-800g/1½-2lbs salmon tailpiece, filleted into two triangles
1 heaped tbls sea salt
1 rounded tbls sugar
1 teaspoon crushed black peppercorns
1 tbls brandy (optional)
1 heaped tbls fresh dill
Mix all the pickling ingredients and put some of the mixture into a flat dish. Put one piece of salmon skinside down and spread more of the mixture over the cut side. Now put the second piece of salmon cutside down and spread the remaining mixture on top, rubbing it well into the skin. Cover the salmon with kitchen foil and press the salmon down with a weighted board or a couple of heavy cans. Leave in a cool place for at least 12 hours or up to 5 days. When ready to serve, slice the salmon thinly and serve with buttered rye bread. A mustard and dill mayonnaise is usually served with this dish.

IDENTIFICATION

Height 60-75cm (2-2½ft), spread 30cm (12in)
Root thin white tap-root, spindle-shaped, 23-30cm (9-12in) long
Stem erect, single, green, hollow, smooth
Leaf green, upper ones linear and thread-like, lower leaflets broader, though still very narrow, sheathing leaf stems
Flower tiny, in flattened umbel-clusters June-July
Seed in this case the fruit, biscuit-coloured ridged, flat, oval, freely produced, bitter-tasting; viable 3 years

pickled salmon & mustard sauce

dried dill flower & leaves

dill seeds

dill leaves

Elder

The elder or elderberry is a very old herbal plant indeed, with hundreds of uses. It is a native of Europe, western Asia and North Africa, and its wide distribution throughout the hedgerows of Europe and general usefulness have resulted in its gathering a vast quantity of legends, magical beliefs and superstitions. Planting it outside the backdoor was a sure way of keeping witches out of the house, and it was thought never to be struck by lightning; cutting it brought bad luck, and traditionally it was the wood of the Cross of Calvary. Pipes can be made from the branches for music, possibly the origin of the Pan-pipes, and throughout Europe it was an important and much used plant until the present day. American elder (*Sambucus canadensis*) is a closely related species and was widely used by American Indians as a folk medicine.
Cultivation The elder grows very rapidly indeed, and self-sows freely, to produce new shoots 120cm (4ft) long in one season; it will flower within three years from seed and often sooner. Hardwood cuttings put outdoors in autumn are another method of increase. Sun or shade and most soils are suitable, though it will flower best in sun, and has a preference for moist soil. It is not a particularly decorative plant, even in flower, but there is a golden-leaved garden form, *S.n.* 'Aurea', which makes a good splash through spring and summer.

IDENTIFICATION

Height usually about 3m (10ft) tall, but can be small tree to 10m (30ft), spread 2.4m (8ft) plus
Root deeply penetrating, fibrous and anchoring
Stem erect, branching, woody, outside covered with light brown bark, becoming grooved with age
Leaf medium-dark green, five toothed lanceolate leaflets, each 2.5-9cm (1-3½in) long, unpleasantly aromatic
Flower creamy white, tiny, massed in flat-headed clusters, produced in profusion in May-July, fragrant
Seed clusters of wine-black, globe-shaped berries on red stems containing seed, August-September

USES

Culinary flowers, for tea or tisane, fritters, added to jam, jellies, milk puddings and tart fruits, used for elderflower wine and champagne; fruit for wine, elderberry wine, jam, jelly, substitute for capers, for chutney and the juice to flavour vinegar
Medicinal flowers, (fresh and dried), fruit, leaves (fresh and dried), bark and root, for emetics; a tea made with equal parts of peppermint leaf, yarrow and elder flowers plus boiling water is one of the finest cures available for colds, coughs and catarrh; of value for rheumatism, sciatica, and cystitis
Cosmetic elderflower water for whitening and softening the skin; to remove freckles, for tonic facepacks, and eye lotions
Domestic a fly repellent; gives a lavender or violet dye with alum
Fragrance and Aroma flowers fragrant, leaves strongly aromatic when bruised

PRESCRIPTION

Elderberry conserve (for neuralgias and migraine)
400g/1lb elderberries
400g/1lb sugar
To make the conserve, boil elder fruit (the berries) with the least quantity of water to produce a pulp. Pass through a sieve and simmer the juice gently to remove most of the water. Add the white sugar, and stir constantly until the consistency of a conserve is produced. Pour into a suitable clean glass container. Take 2 teaspoons as required.

Elderflower sorbet (Recipe on page 138/9)

elderberry conserve

dried elderflower

elderflower sorbet

elder leaves & berries

Fennel

A full-grown plant of fennel makes a delightfully feathery green addition to a herbaceous border, lightening other, heavier and denser blocks of foliage; there is a form with bronze leaves to provide an agreeable addition to a red border or amongst silvery-leaved plants. It is a native of the Mediterranean region, especially near the sea.

As with most herbs, it was used by the canny and resourceful Romans and Greeks for medicinal and culinary purposes. It was illustrated in a 15th century manuscript, and Gerard referred to it as being useful for preserving the eyesight; Culpeper advised its use for those 'that are bit with serpents or have eat . . . mushrooms'. It was thought in mediaeval times to have magic associations and was hung over doors on Midsummer's Eve to ward off evil spirits. Through all the beliefs and countries which used it runs the thread of its curative effect on the eyes, and ability to strengthen the sight. The seeds chewed prevent a feeling of hunger, so would appear to be an excellent weight-reducer. **Cultivation** Fennel can be grown from seed sown in spring where it is to remain. Seedlings should be thinned to 45cm (18in) spacing. If need be, established plants can be divided, and the divisions planted, also in spring. It should not be grown near to dill, otherwise the two will cross-fertilize, to produce seed which is neither one nor the other. Well-drained soil and a sunny sheltered place are important. Florence fennel (*finocchio*) is the vegetable fennel with a bulbous base to the main stem.

USES

Culinary fresh or dried leaf with fish dishes, salad, and salad dressings, yoghurt and fat meats; seeds may also be used; root and stems eaten as a vegetable
Medicinal dried seeds and fresh or dried leaf, used for flatulence, in gripe waters; has some diuretic effect
Cosmetic a decoction of the leaves for eye strain; infusion of the leaves for inflamed eyelids, as part of a facepack to smooth and soften skin
Domestic not so used
Fragrance and Aroma all parts strongly aromatic, especially the leaves and seeds, a mixture of aniseed and a distinctive aroma of its own

RECIPE

Grilled trout with fennel
Fennel leaves add distinction to any fish dish and salmon, mackerel or red mullet can be substituted for trout in this recipe.
4 fresh trout (1 per person)
2 tbls chopped fennel leaves
50g/2oz/¼ cup melted butter
Clean the fish if this has not already been done, and open them out flat. Sprinkle the inside with chopped fennel, close them up and brush them with melted butter. Lay sprigs of fresh fennel on foil on the grill rack, and put the trout on top, sprinkle them with chopped fennel. Grill each side for about 4-5 minutes, and serve with a green salad, dry white wine and French bread.

UMBELLIFERAE
Foeniculum vulgare
Herbaceous perennial

IDENTIFICATION

Height 1.5m (5ft), spread 60cm (2ft)
Root creamy or white, tapering, fleshy, like a long carrot
Stem stout, solid until mature, green smooth, jointed
Leaf thread-like and feathery, green, considerably branched
Flower bright yellow, tiny, in large umbel clusters, mid-late summer
Seed light brown, flat, oval, ridged, 6-12mm (¼-½in) long, August-September

fennel seeds

Florentine fennel

fennel leaves

trout with fennel

dried fennel stalk

| LEGUMINOSAE *Trigonella foenum-graecum*
Half-hardy annual

Fenugreek

One of the oldest fodder herbs known, fenugreek has been used to feed cattle round the countries bordering the Mediterranean for thousands of years. In fact, the specific name is the Latin for Greek hay, and as the flavour is popular with livestock, it is often added to encourage the eating of unfamiliar foods.

It is not unlike lucerne, also a fodder crop, and used similarly, mainly in veterinary medicine rather than human medicine. However, it is still used in cooking, as a spice and a flavouring, especially the seeds, by the Indians and Egyptians. It has also been found to be a source of one of the major ingredients of the contraceptive pill.

Cultivation Fenugreek is a native of southern Europe and Asia, so is grown commercially in Morocco, India, Egypt and elsewhere in Africa. It is quite hardy, and must be sown under cover, with warmth, in March in Britain and North America or sown outdoors in May with protection. Spacing should be about 23cm (9in), and it needs plenty of sun and well-drained but fertile soil. In favourable summers a good crop of seed is set.

IDENTIFICATION

Height 60cm (2ft), spread 23cm (9in)
Root fibrous, bearing nodules
Stem smooth, green, erect, somewhat branching to make a bushy plant
Leaf trefoil, serrated, on stems, alternate
Flower pale yellow to white pea-flower, single or paired, April-June
Seed light brown, pods beaked, 20-50cm (10-20in) long, narrow, slightly curved

fenugreek seeds

USES

Culinary as one of the many kinds of sprouting seeds, eaten when germinated seeds are a few cm tall; lightly roasted ground seeds used in curry; also used in Middle Eastern sweets such as halva; fresh leaves used in curry dishes
Medicinal seed can be used for flatulence, or as a poultice for skin inflammations
Cosmetic not so used
Domestic seed provides a yellow dye
Fragrance and Aroma bitterly aromatic, ground seeds have odour of coumarin, similar to newly mown hay

PRESCRIPTION

Fenugreek water (for dyspepsia or diarrhoea)
The celery-flavoured seeds form the part of the herb of medicinal importance. Almost one-third of these consist of a mucilaginous substance which is of great benefit to inflamed conditions of the digestive tract associated with dyspepsia and diarrhoea.

To make Fenugreek water simmer 35g/1oz of seeds with 600ml/1 pint/2½ cups of water in a covered pan for 15 minutes. Allow to cool and drink a wineglassful.

fenugreek water

sprouting fenugreek seeds

Feverfew

The common name is a corruption of the word febrifuge, from the Latin *febis*, fever, and *fugo*, put to flight, but it does not seem in the past to have been used or considered a specific remedy for high temperatures. Gerard advised use of the dried plant for those 'that are giddie in the head or which have the turning called Vertigo. Also it is good for such as be melancholike and pensive . . .' Culpeper advised it as being 'very effectual for all pains in the head coming of a cold cause', and modern research seems to indicate fairly conclusively that chewing the fresh leaves daily has considerable help in curing migraine.

It is a pretty flowering plant, rather bushy in habit, native of south-eastern Europe, and now naturalized widely in the rest of Europe and North America, growing anywhere which is well-drained. The whole plant is strongly aromatic, rather bitter; it is not a bee plant, but in spite of that seed sets well. **Cultivation** Feverfew will seed itself readily once there is a plant in the garden, in particular where the drainage is good and the sun plentiful; it will root in walls and between cracks in paving. It remains green and leafy through the winter. A garden form is called 'White Bonnets' in which there is doubling of the white petals, with a greenish yellow centre, and hybrids are often found, intermediate between the two, with yellow centres and more, or less, white petals. The yellow-leaved form, *C. p.* 'Aurea' is low-growing and good for edgings, particularly conspicuous in winter. Increase may also be by division of the plant.

USES

Culinary not so used
Medicinal fresh or dried leaves, whole plant fresh or dried, flowers fresh or dried; for headaches and migraine, as a tonic, and to ward off biting insects
Cosmetic as an ingredient of creams for the skin
Domestic as a moth repellent
Fragrance and Aroma strongly and bitterly aromatic

PRESCRIPTION

Feverfew salad (for migraine)
This common weed of the daisy family has recently received close scientific attention which has proved the claim of its effectiveness in the treatment of migraine conditions. One fresh leaf per day eaten in a sandwich or salad is all that should be taken. A few individuals may experience a body and arm rash when taking this herb, particularly if other chemical drugs have also been prescribed. In such cases consult your doctor.

COMPOSITAE
Chrysanthemum parthenium
Herbaceous perennial

IDENTIFICATION

Height 45-60cm (18-24in), spread 45cm (18in)
Root fibrous, spreading
Stem erect, branched, slightly downy, green
Leaf light green, about 8cm (3 in) long, and as much wide, twice pinnate with the edges of the leaflets deeply cut and toothed, giving a feathery appearance, leaf-stem flat above, convex beneath, alternate
Flower daisy-like, white ray-petals, yellow centre nearly flat in clusters, profusely produced, June-October, later in mild autumns
Seed tiny, light brown, without a pappus

feverfew leaves

feverfew seeds

salad with feverfew

Garlic

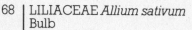

IDENTIFICATION

Height flowering stem 40-60cm (12-24in)

Root a bulb made up of several cloves enclosed in a white papery skin; cloves are white to pinkish and are, botanically, swollen leaves which have evolved as storage organs; attached to the base of the bulb are a cluster of fibrous true roots

Stem green, smooth, round

Leaf flat, linear, pointed at the tip, long, from the base, or up the flowering stem

Flower white to pink in a round head, mixed with bulbils, the whole enclosed in a papery white skin soon bursting open, July-August

Seed black

garlic cloves

Garlic's popularity in Britain has increased tenfold in recent years, but it has always been an ingredient of Continental cooking, and is now also becoming an essential part of many North American dishes. The flavour of the cloves is pungent, highly individual and long-lasting – its presence in food is unmistakable, and its action on the stomach and intestine is considerable, since it has powerful antiseptic properties. Any tendency towards constipation is rapidly cured.

Garlic was probably originally indigenous to Asia, but it now grows widely wherever there is a warm climate, and it is perfectly hardy in northern Europe and North America though the flavour is less good in cooler latitudes. Its use is so long-standing as to be recorded at least 5,000 years ago – in Sumeria. It was certainly grown by the Anglo-Saxons, as the name is derived from *gar*, a lance, and *leac*, a leek, both Anglo-Saxon words, referring (depending on your authority) to the shape of the leaves, the tips of the cloves or the stem.

In mediaeval Britain it was eaten in very large quantities, often raw, and a few centuries later William Shakespeare commented unfavourably on its smell. However, cooked garlic eaten in discreet quantities is quite acceptable. As a flavouring garlic has no equal, and it is an integral part of all the top cuisines of the world.

Cultivation Garlic can quite well be grown in cool temperate climates and is hardy, but the flavour may not be as good as that grown in warmer, drier countries. The site chosen for it should be as sunny, well-drained and as warm as possible, preferably hot. Cloves can be planted in October, to get ahead with the growth, or in early April; plant them 15-20cm (6-8in) apart and about 2.5cm (1in) deep, i.e. with 2.5cm (1in) of soil above the tip of the clove. Grow in fertile soil, and if need be, mix in a little really well-rotted garden compost sometime before planting, together with a scattering of a general organic fertilizer. Give a light nitrogenous feed in spring and finish the plants with potash dressing in early summer. They will be mature in July-August when the top growth starts to change colour and keel over. Plants rarely flower in cool climates; tying the stems in a knot is said to increase the size of the cloves.

dried minced garlic

aioli

garlic bread

garlic butter

garlic leaves

USES

Culinary ripe cloves have innumerable uses, preferably crushed, in all kinds of savoury cooking, but especially with meat, fish and vegetables; fondues, omelettes, salads, flans, sauces; if frying, do so lightly – too hot oil or fat destroys the good flavour

Medicinal cloves have antiseptic properties; of help in catarrh, bronchitis, colds, for wounds, infectious diseases such as typhoid, as a diuretic, and an expectorant

Cosmetic can control dandruff

Domestic said to control garden aphids and ward off black spot from roses

Fragrance and Aroma pungently aromatic, unpleasantly so in quantity or if grown in cool conditions

RECIPE

Aioli (garlic mayonnaise)
This classic Provençal sauce is traditionally served with poached or boiled fish although in some parts of Provence it makes an unusual but excellent accompaniment to roast or grilled lamb.
4-6 cloves (depending on size of cloves and how much you like garlic)
2 egg yolks
300ml/½ pint/1¼ cups olive oil
salt and pepper
1 tbls lemon juice
Pound the cloves with the salt and pepper until smooth, then add the egg yolks, blending in well with a wooden spoon. Add the oil very carefully, drop by drop, beating in between each drop to avoid curdling until about a quarter has been added, then mix in the rest, pouring it in slowly and beating at the same time. Finally, add lemon juice. Once thick enough, use as a dip, or to accompany salad, fish, fish soup, vegetables or eggs.

Garlic bread (Recipe on page 138/9)

garlic bulb

sliced crushed garlic cloves

GERANIACEAE
Pelargonium spp.
Half-hardy herbaceous
perennial

Geranium
Scented-leaved

The scented-leaved geraniums constitute a different group of plants to the hardy kinds grown outdoors as border perennials, which are species of the genus *Geranium*. They are related to the greenhouse 'geraniums' or pelargoniums and, like them, need protection against cold.

Nearly all the species come from the Cape, South Africa, and amongst the first to be discovered and brought to England was *P. triste*, one of the very few whose flowers rather than leaves are scented. It was Charles I's gardener Tradescant who found it, and there followed a steady stream of pelargoniums renowned for their fragrant or aromatic foliage. What is extraordinary about this group is the tremendous variation in perfumes and aromas: *P. tomentosum* is strongly peppermint-scented, its soft leaves covered with fine, silky hairs; *P.* 'Clorinda', eucalyptus-scented; 'Attar of Roses', *P. graveolens* and *P. radens* rose-scented; *P. abrotanifolium*, southernwood; *P. odoratissimum*, apple-scented; *P. crispum minor*, lemon-scented; oak-leaf *P. quercifolium*, incense and *P. fragrans*, nutmeg-scented. Not surprisingly, the main use of these geraniums is in perfumery.

Cultivation The scented-leaved pelargoniums need well-drained potting compost or soil, and plenty of sun and warmth. They can be grown outdoors in cool temperate climates from June-September, but will need protection the remainder of the time. Under cover they will flower from May-November. In winter they should be encouraged to rest by lowering the temperature and keeping the compost almost dry. In late winter they should be cut back hard to leave a few cm (in) of stem, otherwise they can become rather straggly. Increase is by tip cuttings taken during spring-summer under cover.

IDENTIFICATION

Height in the range 23-90cm (9-36in)
Root mostly fibrous, *P. triste* tuberous
Stem smooth, erect, branching, tending to be woody at the base
Leaf generally smooth, opposite, much divided in some varieties, others palmate with large rounded lobes
Flower small, in clusters, each with 5 petals, the 2 upper being larger, sometimes differently coloured; colours shades of red, pink, purple, lavender, maroon or white
Seed pod is a long pointed beak containing tiny black seeds

USES

Culinary fresh leaves for milk puddings, custards, jellies; fruit, summer fruit drinks, ice cream, and cakes
Medicinal not so used
Cosmetic essential oil (geraniol) for washing or bathing
Domestic amongst household linen and clothing for perfumery and insect repellent
Fragrance and Aroma leaves of varying odours as above used in potpourri, sachets, and tussie-mussies; essential oils in perfumery

RECIPE

Rose geranium punch
1 litre/2 pints/5 cups apple juice
4 limes
200g/8oz/1 cup sugar
6 leaves rose-scented geranium
6 drops green vegetable colouring (optional)
Boil the apple juice, sugar and geranium leaves for 5 minutes. Add thinly sliced and crushed limes. Cool, strain and add colouring. Pour on to ice in glasses and garnish with geranium petals.
Rose geranium butter
Butter pounded with the leaves makes a delicious spread for cake fillings, on sweet biscuits and spread on bread slices topped with apple jelly.

rose geranium punch

rose geranium leaves

rose geranium butter

rose geranium oil

Honeysuckle

OTHER NAMES: Woodbine

Very much a plant of northern Europe including Britain, honeysuckle can also be found growing wild in North Africa and western Asia. Although it seems unlikely, it does have a history of herbal use, being listed in Gerard's herbal; 'the floures steeped in oil and set in the Sun, are good to anoint the body that is benummed, and growne very cold'. Culpeper regarded it as 'a hot martial plant in the sign of Cancer, the leaves being put into gargarisms for sore throats', and it was another of Dioscorides' plants for curing the hiccups.

It is, of course, grown above all for its fragrance, and was one of those flowers listed by Francis Bacon in his essay 'Of Gardens' whose 'breath' is 'far sweeter in the air than in the hand', honeysuckles being included in the list, 'so they be somewhat afar off'.

Cultivation Honeysuckle likes its feet in the shade and head in the sunshine; grown in too sunny or too warm a place, it becomes infested with greenfly, blackfly, caterpillars and red spider mite. Ordinary soil, reasonably moist and fertile, with an alkaline tendency, will be suitable, and a position against a north or west wall is ideal, or on the shady side of supports such as tree stumps, poles and pergolas. It will twine round its support, after being directed towards it. Planting is in autumn-spring, and increase is by hardwood cuttings in autumn, or by layering late summer, autumn. If pruning is needed, do this in early spring.

honeysuckle leaves & flowers

honeysuckle syrup
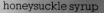

IDENTIFICATION

Height 3-6m (10-20ft)
Root fibrous, anchoring, wide-spreading
Stem twining, tough, rambling over bushes, up hedgerows and trees
Leaf oval to oblong, simple, entire, in pairs, upper ones stalkless but not united, dark green, 4-6cm (1½-2½in) long
Flower creamy yellow, purplish on the outside, long slender tube 5cm (2in), ending in 2-lobed lip 2.5cm (1in) wide, very sweetly fragrant, in clusters at the end of shoots, June-October
Seed cream-coloured, contained in globe-shaped red berries

USES

Culinary flowers formerly used as soothing syrup
Medicinal flowering plant, for skin infections; berries are *poisonous*
Cosmetic not so used
Domestic not so used
Fragrance and Aroma flowers strongly scented, for potpourri, herb pillows and perfumery

PRESCRIPTION

Syrup of honeysuckle (for the relief of a sore throat)
This is a modern version of a recipe in *A New Family Herbal* by Richard Brooks, 1871.
75g/3oz/2¼ cups fresh honeysuckle petals
300ml/½ pint/1¼ cups boiling water
100g/4oz/½ cup sugar
Lightly crush the honeysuckle leaves before pouring boiling water over them. Leave to get cool, then strain the liquid into a saucepan. Add the sugar and bring slowly to the boil. Leave to simmer gently until the mixture is of a syrupy consistency. Cool slightly, then pour into a bottle or jar and seal.

| CRUCIFERAE *Armoracia rusticana*, syn. *Cochlearia armoracia*
Herbaceous perennial

Horseradish

Culinary raw or dried root for sauce with meat, especially beef; in vinegar; as an accompaniment grated or powdered (dried) to any meat, sausages, ham, vegetables and fish dishes; adds spice to egg dishes
Medicinal fresh root, use with care on boils and for bronchitis, coughs and as a stimulant, but large quantities can be harmful both externally and internally
Cosmetic not so used
Domestic not so used
Fragrance and Aroma roots pungently aromatic when bruised

IDENTIFICATION

Height flowering stem about 60cm (2ft), spread to 90cm (3ft)
Root large, fleshy, white, many thick branches deeply penetrating
Stem erect, leafy, with long-stemmed flower spikes along it
Leaf basal leaves in a rosette, each large, shiny, oblong, slightly toothed, 30-50cm (12-32in) long; stem leaves narrow, pointed, toothed or deeply cut, alternate
Flower white, tiny, scented, many in a loose spike with several spikes on a stem, late spring-summer
Seed Black

The prefix 'horse' in many plant names does not mean that the plant is a particularly delectable food as far as those animals are concerned; it did in fact evolve from 'coarse', and in this case served to separate the plant from the one which actually supplied a radish root. Horsechestnut is a similar case.

The hot-tasting fleshy roots have probably been used for at least 3,000 years as a food flavouring and, although it is native to eastern Europe, it grows wild in northern Europe including Britain, and North America. It was much used in Germany and Denmark as an alternative to mustard during the Middle Ages. Gerard says that pounded and mixed with vinegar it was used by the Germans as a sauce for fish and with 'such like meates as we do mustard'. It had some medicinal use as well, but was not much eaten in Britain until the 17th century.

Cultivation The problem in cultivating horseradish is not so much how to make it grow well, as to curb its enthusiasm and stop it taking over the garden. However, to obtain the juiciest and most succulent roots, use root cuttings about 1.2cm (½in) wide and 20cm (8in) long, and plant in February-March, making sure that each has a bud. Remove the sideroots, and plant in holes 30cm (12in) deep, 45cm (18in) apart. Deep moist soils are preferable and any site. After two seasons the quality will start to deteriorate, and replanting will be necessary a year or two later. When digging up the plants, remove every piece of root, otherwise it will sprout again.

horseradish cream

grated horseradish root

horseradish root

horseradish leaves

RECIPE

Horseradish cream
A traditional sauce for hot and cold
roast beef and for all kinds of
smoked fish. In Germany, this is also
a popular sauce with asparagus.
300ml/¹/₂ pint/1¹/₄ cups thick cream
1¹/₂-2 tbls grated horseradish
1-2 teaspoons lemon juice
salt, ground pepper and a little
sugar to taste.
Gradually add grated horseradish to
the cream until you have the desired
hotness. Add lemon juice, salt,
pepper and sugar to taste.

Horsetail

Unlikely though it seems the horsetails are plants left over from prehistoric times, having survived almost unchanged for hundreds of millions of years, judging by the evidence of fossil remains. They do not flower, but carry spores, as ferns do, to which they are related, and have clusters of frond-like branches on erect stems, the appearance of which has given them their common name; they are sometimes also called mare's-tails.

The fronds have a harsh feel to them and this is because the plants, uniquely, absorb large quantities of silica from the soil. As a result they were used as pot-scourers, especially the species *E. hyemale*, called Dutch rush or scouring rush, and used in Britain and North America for cleaning and polishing metal such as pewter, brass and copper, and for scouring wooden containers and milk-pails.

Cultivation If horsetail is to be introduced to the garden at all, it is best confined to a container or, if planted in the open, in an area of the soil bounded by concrete at sides and bottom, so that the rhizomes cannot penetrate what in effect is a concrete box. In the open ground, unconfined, horsetail becomes a permanent inhabitant, only eradicated with great difficulty. Its 'root' system has been found to extend down the face of a cliff 12m (40ft), and breaking the rhizomes stimulates buds on the remainder to sprout and produce more growth and spores. The top growth dies down completely in winter.

IDENTIFICATION

Height 20-60cm (8-24in), spread 20cm (8in)
Root rhizome or creeping underground stem, with fibrous roots attached, brown, tough, jointed, extremely deeply and widely penetrating
Stem two kinds: fertile are brown, about 20cm (8in) long, sheathed at the joints; infertile are green, jointed, 30-60cm (12-24in) long, whorls of branches at the joints, furrowed
Leaf a small scale, arranged in whorls which are fused to form a tubular sheath surrounding the stem
Flower none as such, but fertile stems have brown cone-like spike on tips which bear the spores
Seed none, the spore is the equivalent, a single-celled microscopic organism, powder-like when shed in quantity

USES

Culinary young shoots once used in salads; green stems as a vegetable, prepared like asparagus; eaten fried with flour and butter
Medicinal dried or fresh barren stems used as poultice for healing wounds, and to stop bleeding; will reduce the swelling of eyelids; a diuretic and effective in incontinence
Cosmetic as a strengthener, and to remove the white spots that occur on nails; also for strengthening the hair, and as an astringent and toner for skin
Domestic supplies a dye, as the colour grey with alum
Fragrance and Aroma none

PRESCRIPTION

Horsetail nail strengthener
Horsetail contains more of the element silicon, available in water soluble forms, than almost any other plant, and is the pre-eminent herb for the promotion of strength and lustre to hair and nails.

A simple method of improving easily-broken nails is to immerse the fingertips in a decoction made by simmering 50g/2oz of the dry herb in 900ml/1½ pints/3¾ cups of water for 20 minutes.

dried horsetail

horsetail nail strengthener

horsetail stems & leaves

Hyssop

The somewhat bitter though minty flavour of hyssop leaves has given them a mixed reception amongst cooks and gourmets, so it is not surprising that hyssop's original use was medicinal, as suggested by the specific name – *officinalis* (from the Latin *officina*, workshop) indicates that the plant was authorized for use by the medical profession and could be sold in pharmacies.

Native of central and southern Europe, and western Asia, it is also found in temperate regions of North America. It is an inhabitant of rocky ground. It occurs naturally in Palestine, but the hyssop of the Bible is thought to be either marjoram or the caper plant (*Capparis spinosa*). Gerard said that 'all kinds of Hyssope do grow in my Garden' and disdained to describe it, any more than Dioscorides did: 'as being a plant so well known that it needed none' (description), and it was illustrated in an Italian Herbal published in 1744, where it was called *H. vulgaris*. It was once a country remedy for rheumatism, using the fresh green tops made into a tea, and Culpeper recommended it as an excellent medicine for the 'quinsy . . . to gargle it, when boiled with figs'.

Cultivation Hyssop is easily grown in as sunny a place as possible, and dry, well-drained soil. Plant in spring about 30cm (12in) apart, growing it from divisions, seed sown in spring, or tip cuttings taken before it flowers. Protect in severe winters, and replace every four or five years. It can be clipped lightly to keep it formal in early spring.

USES

Culinary fresh leaves sparingly in salads; with strongly flavoured meat, in soup, sausages, in fruit recipes; an ingredient of Chartreuse liqueur
Medicinal fresh leaves, dried flowering tops, for colds, bronchitis, as a gargle for sore throats, to encourage appetite; to heal bruises, black eyes and swellings
Cosmetic not so used
Domestic fresh or dried leaves as strewing herb, in moth sachets, as a flea-repellent and in water for washing, whether self or clothing
Fragrance and Aroma stems, flowers, leaves strongly aromatic, slightly bitter, hot and mint-like; for aromatic candles, potpourri; oil used in perfumery

PRESCRIPTION

Hyssop gargle (for sore throats)
Hyssop contains almost one per cent of an essential oil whose medicinal action is very similar to that of garden sage.

A strong infusion made with 50g/2oz of hyssop to 600ml/1 pint/2½ cups of water makes an excellent home remedy for sore throats when used as a gargle. The penicillin-producing mold grows naturally on the herb's leaves and also adds to the antibiotic effect of the plant.
Hyssop treatment (for bruising around the eyes)
In addition, hyssop is an excellent treatment for bruising around the eyes; crush a handful of fresh leaves into a clean handerchief, dip this quickly into boiling water, and apply locally as hot as it can be tolerated. Repeat until the swelling subsides.

LABIATAE *Hyssopus officinalis*
Sub-shrub

IDENTIFICATION

Height in cultivation 30-60cm (12-24in), spread 20-30cm (8-12in)
Root mainly fibrous
Stem tough, woody, low down brown, green and angular higher up, branched
Leaf narrow, dark green, pointed, to 2.5cm (1in) long and 2mm (⅛in) wide, opposite
Flower pale blue, pink or white, tubular, 2-lipped, about 6mm (¼in) long, in long narrow spikes, July-October
Seed tiny, brown

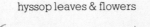
hyssop leaves & flowers

hyssop eye treatment

dried hyssop leaves

LABIATAE *Lavandula angustifolia*, syn. *L. officinalis, L. vera*
Evergreen shrub

IDENTIFICATION

Height 60-90cm (2-3ft), spread 60-75cm (2-2½ft)
Root mostly fibrous, spreading, shallow
Stem short, woody, grey flaking bark, much branched
Leaf grey-green, narrow, entire, up to 5cm (2in) long, 2mm (⅛in) wide, stalkless, opposite
Flower lavender-purple, 2-lipped tubular, 6mm (¼in) long, produced in blunt spikes up to 5cm (2in) long, July-November (mainly July)
Seed black, tiny

lavender seeds

Lavender

It would be difficult to find a more well-known or generally more well-loved fragrance than that of lavender. It is a native plant of the Mediterranean *maquis*, that area on the hillsides of dry, rocky soil, exposed to blazing sun, with little rainfall, and that mainly in winter, which is host to herbs, sub-shrubs, bulbs and quickly-seeding annuals. Lavender's use can be traced back to the Greeks and Romans and it is more than likely that it was used all round the Mediterranean by Egyptians, Arabs, and Sumerians for a variety of domestic, cosmetic and perfumery needs. It is extremely probable that it was one of the many plants brought over to Britain by the Roman occupationary army to remind the legionaries, while they shivered in the damp foggy cold, of the warmth and dryness they had left behind at home.

'Who'll buy my lavender?' is a street-cry within living memory, and bunches of lavender are still occasionally sold from door to door in English villages and country districts. In England, lavender was grown commercially until the last war in Surrey and in Kent; now it is only grown in Norfolk, near Norwich. In North America, it grows best in warm dry regions.

Cultivation Lavender is slightly tender, and will be better able to survive if grown in a warm sunny position and dry, well-drained soil so that it ripens and matures thoroughly before winter. Grow from tip cuttings taken with a heel in spring or late summer, and plant in May. Space the plants 60cm (2ft) apart each way; as a hedge allow 30-45cm (12-18in). Harvest the flower spikes for drying just as the flowers begin to unfold. Any trimming should be done in mid-spring, very lightly so as not to cut into growth older than that produced the previous year. Remove flower stems in the first year for a stronger bushier plant.

USES

Culinary not generally used, though could be tried in jellies, crystallized in confectionary, and with strongly flavoured meats such as venison or pheasant
Medicinal dried flowers, oil; as antiseptic, a restorative for faintness, for relieving sprains, or rheumatic pain
Cosmetic in water for washing and bathing, as an astringent for the skin
Domestic to repel household insects; to relieve insect bites, and to ward off mosquitoes, midges and so on
Fragance and Aroma flowerheads and flowers strongly and sweetly scented; used in potpourri, as perfume, in furniture polish, candles, to perfume rinsing water for hair and in sleep pillows

RECIPE

Lavender oil (for after the bath)
300ml/½ pint/1¼ cups almond oil fresh lavender flowers
Put oil into a clear glass bottle, then add spikes of lavender flowers, picked just as they are about to open. Put in as many as the bottle will hold conveniently, and put it in a warm sunny place for 12 hours, and keep warm for the next 12, then remove the spikes. If the oil is not fragrant enough, repeat the process until it is. Then stopper firmly and store in a cool dark place when not in use. The keeping qualities will be improved if one-tenth of the oil is replaced with wheatgerm oil.

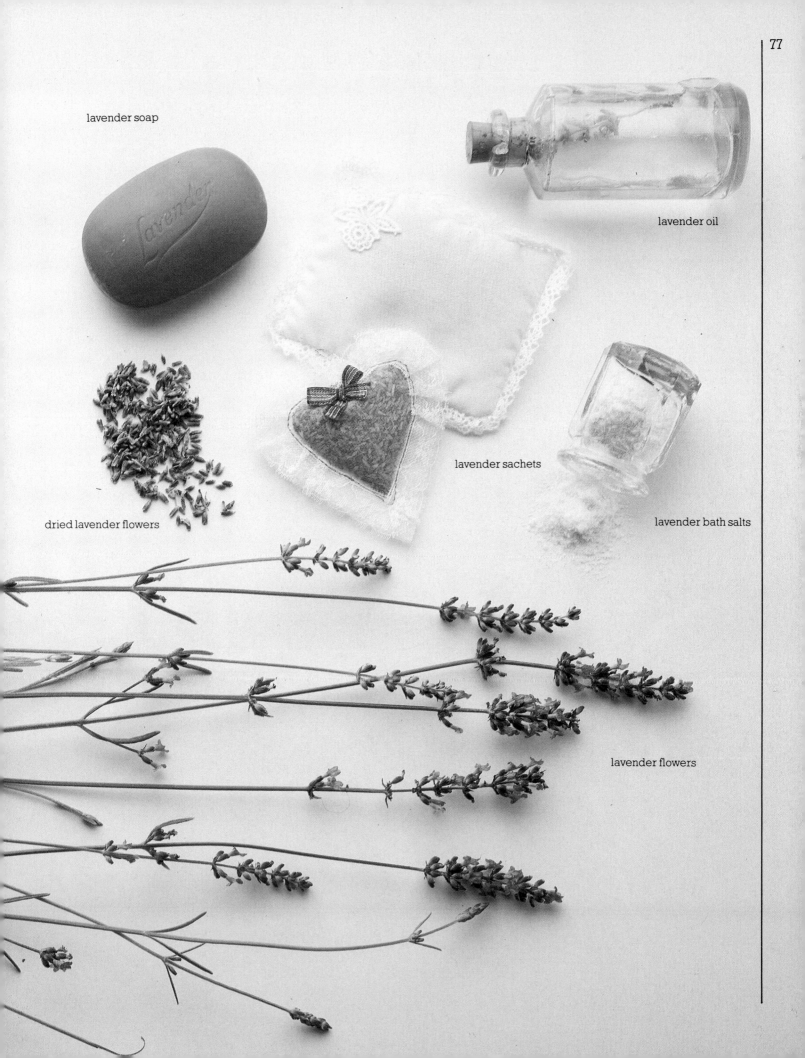

lavender soap

lavender oil

dried lavender flowers

lavender sachets

lavender bath salts

lavender flowers

VERBENACEAE *Aloysia triphylla*, syn. *Lippia citriodora*
Tender deciduous shrub

LemonVerbena

IDENTIFICATION

Height average in cultivation 1.8m (6ft), spread 1.2-1.5m (4-5ft), but may be much less in cool gardens, or much more where sheltered and mild
Root fibrous and anchor roots
Stem angular, green skin to brown bark with maturity, woody, erect, gracefully branching
Leaf green, lanceolate, long-pointed to 10cm (4in) long, 2.5cm (1in) wide, produced in threes, hairs on margins
Flower pale purple, 2-lipped tubular, 1.2cm (½in) long, in spike-like clusters, August
Seed brown

Not to be confused with vervain, also verbena (*V. officinalis*), lemon verbena is quite different in appearance since it is a shrub and not a herbaceous plant from South America, specifically Chile. Its lemon fragrance is given off by the leaves without the need to rub them, unlike lemon balm and, even when dried, continue to be pungently scented for years, so that they constitute an excellent ingredient for potpourris. If lemon verbena was not inclined to be tender in cool temperate climates, it would be in every herb garden or wherever perfume is valued by the gardener.
Cultivation Lemon verbena needs protection in most parts of cool temperate climates so that the winter temperature does not fall below 4°C (40°F). In mild sheltered sites, it will survive outdoors all year. If outdoors, use a proprietary potting compost and a container at least 30cm (12in) diameter. Remove dead tips and shoots in early spring, and prune to control the growth at the same time. Plant outdoors in spring, and take soft cuttings in July under cover in sandy compost.

vanilla & lemon ice cream

USES

Culinary fresh or dried leaves used sparingly for fish, salads, stuffing for chicken, pork, in puddings, with ice cream, mushroom dishes
Medicinal fresh or dried leaves for indigestion and flatulence, as a mild sedative
Cosmetic to perfume water for bathing or washing, as a freshener for skin in soaps
Domestic sachets for bed-linen and clothing
Fragrance and Aroma strongly lemon-scented leaves, long-lasting; for potpourri, sweet-smelling pillow, or tussy-mussie; the oil is used in perfumery

RECIPE

Vanilla and lemon ice cream
150ml/¼ pint/⅔ cup milk
50g/2oz/¼ cup sugar
2 egg yolks, beaten
½ tspn vanilla essence
150ml/¼ pint/⅔ cup double cream
1 teaspoon chopped fresh lemon verbena leaves
Partially beat the cream. Make a custard with the milk, sugar and beaten egg yolks, by heating the milk and sugar, then pouring on to the egg yolks, stirring constantly. Return to the saucepan and heat very slowly, stirring constantly until the mixture becomes thick; too much heat too soon will curdle it. Strain, and add the vanilla, allow to cool, fold in the verbena and partially whipped cream, pour into icecube tray and freeze

lemon verbena leaves

dried lemon verbena leaves

Lovage

One of the attributes of a good witch was to be able to brew love potions on demand, and lovage acquired its name because it was once thought to be an aphrodisiac and was therefore an essential ingredient of such recipes. It is a handsome plant, one of the tallest of the umbelliferous herbs, with a strong distinctive, celery-like flavour which has earned it the name of the 'Maggi' herb in Italy. From south Europe, especially the Liguria province of Italy, it is now naturalized in eastern North America, south-west Asia, Germany, France and Scandinavia, and is easily grown in Britain.

Lovage is illustrated as a woodcut in a herbal of 1491, and merits inclusion in Culpeper's list of useful plants, circa 1645, where he advised that the bruised leaves, 'fried in hog's lard, laid hot to any blotch or boil, will quickly break it.' All parts have considerable use in all sorts of ways – it contains, for instance, an appreciable quantity of vitamin C – and was used as a herb in Britain from the earliest monastic times.

Cultivation Lovage needs plenty of room, a deep moist fertile soil and sun or a little shade. It can be grown from seed sown outdoors in spring in a nursery bed, and transplanted in autumn. Root cuttings are also possible, each piece having an eye, and being replanted with the bud 5cm (2in) below the surface. Allow 1.2m (4ft) between the plants and expect them to reach full size in four years. They will die down completely in winter.

USES

Culinary fresh leaves in meat casseroles, soups, salads, vegetables, marinades, or eat as spinach; seeds even stronger, all meats, bread, game, cheeses; shredded roots for soups or boiled without skin for a vegetable
Medicinal fresh or dried whole plant, seed, dried root, diuretic, for flatulence, antiseptic, for sore throats, a digestive
Cosmetic deodorant, use fresh leaves in the bath water, or a decoction of the roots, which are also said to be effective in removing freckles
Domestic not so used
Fragrance and Aroma strong, yeast/celery odour, all parts, especially seeds

RECIPE

Lovage soup
900ml/1½ pint/3¾ cups stock
1 medium onion, sliced
25g/1oz butter
25g/1oz flour
2 dessertspoons chopped fresh lovage leaves
grated nutmeg
croutons
salt and pepper
Fry the onion gently in the butter until soft, add the lovage and continue for one or two more minutes, then mix in the flour, and add the stock gradually, stirring all the time and bring to the boil. Adjust the seasoning, add the nutmeg, and simmer for 10 to 15 minutes. For a smoother texture, stir in single cream just before serving, and float croutons on the surface.

Herbaceous perennial

IDENTIFICATION

Height 1.8m (6ft) plus, spread 1.2-1.5m (4-5ft)
Root thick, to tapering, branching, fleshy, white internally, brown outside, top of root becoming well over 30cm (12in) wide in time
Stem stout, erect, hollow, round, green, ridged
Leaf dark green, shiny, 3-pinnate, each leaflet wedge-shaped and toothed, entire leaf to 60cm (2ft) long or more, 45cm (18in) wide
Flower yellow, tiny, in umbel clusters, June-July
Seed yellow-brown, flat, oval, ridged, in pairs

dried lovage leaves

lovage seeds

lovage leaves

lovage soup

| **RUBIACEAE** *Rubia tinctorum*
Climbing herbaceous perennial

IDENTIFICATION

Height scrambling stems to 2.4m (8ft)
Root thick, fleshy, branched, black skin, red-tinged flesh with yellow core
Stem green, angular, prickly, stiff
Leaf in whorls, up the stem, about 6 in a whorl, each leaf prickly underneath along the midrib, and on the margins, 5-10cm (2-5in) long
Flower tiny, inconspicuous, yellow-green, in loose clusters, June-September
Seed contained in rounded black berry

Madder

Madder has chiefly been grown to supply the colour red, and as it is a native of southern Europe and western Asia, it is not surprising that the shade of red so obtained is called Turkey red. It is one of the most ancient of dye plants, its use being recorded 2,500 years ago, and it is such a strong dye that it will produce a deep pink-brown without a mordant – with alum and tin it supplies red and red-brown.

However, it will yield other colours besides red, depending on the mordant, such as purple, orange, black and lilac. The chemical which supplies the colouring is dihydroscyanthraquinone, also called alizarin; this was found to be a derivative of the hydrocarbon anthracene, from coal-tar. The whole of the synthetic dyeing industry arose from this and subsequently completely replaced natural dyes. The root is the part used, and this is also of importance medicinally.

Cultivation Madder grows naturally in well-drained, even stony sites, and in light woodland; for the best and most extensive roots a deep soil is the most satisfactory. Some support will be needed for the rambling stems. Planting can be done in spring or autumn, and increase is by division, or by seed sown in spring, or early autumn; the wild Madder, *R. peregrina*, may be a variety of it and also contains a pinkish dye.

USES

Culinary not so used
Medicinal root used as diuretic and of considerable help in kidney troubles; an antiseptic
Cosmetic not so used
Domestic roots to provide mainly red dye, and other colours with a variety of mordants for wool and other materials
Fragrance and Aroma not present

HOUSEHOLD USE

To supply reddish dye
Wool is the most suitable fibre for natural dyes, since it takes the colours evenly. A mordant is necessary to fix the dye and to make it colour fast. With madder, use an alum and cream of tartar mordant.
Alum and cream of tartar mordant
To 100g/4oz wool add 25g/1oz alum and 6g/¼oz cream of tartar, and use sufficient soft water to cover the wool (approx 4.5 litres/1 gallon). Dissolve the alum and cream of tartar in a little boiling water, and stir into the remainder. Put to heat, and when warm slide in the wool, thoroughly wetted. Take 1 hour to bring the solution slowly to simmering point, simmer gently for a further hour. Remove the wool and place in the dye bath.
Dye bath
Use 50g/2oz powdered madder root from a dye supplier. Mix to a paste with hard water (add lime or chalk if tap water is soft) and gradually dilute with sufficient water (about 4.5 litres/1 gallon) to just cover 100g/4oz of mordanted wool. Heat the liquid *without* the wool very slowly until lukewarm, then add the wool and take from 1-2 hours to reach simmering point from that stage, then simmer for 10 minutes. Leave the wool in the dye until it cools, rinse the wool, wash it in soapy water, rinse again and hang to dry.

madder leaves

madder dye bath

ground madder root

Marigold

The cottage-garden marigold, not the modern French and African bedding marigolds, was once a culinary and medicinal plant in daily use, as well as a much-loved decorative flower. By Elizabethan times it was familiar in every garden, and frequently referred to in records of the 13th and 14th centuries, although officially it is not supposed to have been introduced until 1573.

It is a native of southern Europe, but perfectly easy to grow in cool temperate climates, and gets its botanical name from the Latin *calends*, 'the first of every month', meaning that it can be in bloom throughout the year. In mediaeval and earlier times it was commonly called 'golds' or 'ruddes'; its present name is a corruption of the Anglo-Saxon *merso-meagalla*, marsh marigold. Gerard has a long dissertation on it in his *Herbal* of 1597, and shows four coloured illustrations of different sorts, which do not seem to be known nowadays. It was obviously very much a part of everyday life, to such an extent that 'in some Grocers and Spice-sellers House, are to be found barrels filled with them (dried petals)' for use in soup and medicinal prescriptions. The petals were also commonly used to colour cheese and butter.

Cultivation Pot marigolds, as they are often known, are easily grown in a sunny place and light soil, being grown from seed sown outdoors in spring. They should be thinned to about 25cm (10in) apart, and will thereafter seed themselves. For the strongest plants and best-sized flowers, grow them in a good loam. Seed is ripe in late summer

USES

Culinary petals, in place of saffron in many recipes, especially rice dishes; soups, eggs, cheese, meat casseroles; custard; puddings, cakes, salads and to make wine, leaves sparingly in salads

Medicinal fresh flowerheads or petals, for healing wounds, and to treat conjunctivitis; leaves said to be a good remedy for the pain of a bee or wasp sting

Cosmetic flowers and leaves, for the skin, as a cream to soothe, heal and nourish, flowers to lighten the hair

Domestic petals supply a pale yellow dye with alum

Fragrance and Aroma bruised leaves have a bitter aroma

PRESCRIPTION

Marigold cream (for scratches and abrasions)
75g/3oz dried marigold flowers
900ml/1½ pints/3¾ cups boiling water
aqueous cream (available from pharmacists)
Make a healing balm by infusing the dried flowers in boiling water for about 1 hour. Then strain the liquid through clean muslin and squeeze out as much of the moisture as possible. Mix one part of the strained infusion with four parts of aqueous cream. Keep refrigerated and use liberally on the arms and legs for gardening scratches and abrasions.

The infusion alone can be taken internally (sweetened with honey) and is good for the complexion, poor circulation and for ulcers. Externally, it can be used for skin lesions, conjunctivitis and leg ulcers.

COMPOSITAE *Calendula officinalis*
Hardy annual

IDENTIFICATION

Height 15-23cm (6-9in), spread 15cm (6in)
Root fibrous
Stem green, erect
Leaf pale green, oblong, pointed or blunt tipped, to 12cm (5in) long, 3.5cm (1½in) wide, slightly hairy
Flower bright orange, or yellow less commonly, yellow centre, double, average 5cm (2in) diameter, May onwards
Seed light brown, without a pappus

RECIPE

Marigold custard
Make a custard in the ordinary way, but add 1 cupful of fresh marigold petals, beaten, to 600ml/1 pint/2½ cups of milk and heat it gently with the remainder of the custard ingredients.

marigold flowerheads

marigold cream

marigold flowers & leaves

dried marigold flowers

marigold seeds

Marjoram, Sweet

Marjoram grows wild in Britain; it is *O. vulgare*, the same species found in Europe, and called oregano in Italy. But the Italian form has a better flavour, and is to be preferred to the British native, though that can still be used for cooking. The flavour and aroma of sweet marjoram, although characteristically a marjoram, is appreciably different, and a third, pot marjoram (*O. onites*), also used for cooking, has the advantage that it is a hardy perennial, though its flavour is much less attractive than that of the other two.

Sweet marjoram is perennial in its native habitat of central Europe, but is not frost hardy, though it will survive well into late autumn outdoors in a sheltered place. It has innumerable culinary uses and has some medicinal use – it contains thymol – though the wild species has greater application to health. The plant from Crete called dittany is *O. dictamnus*, a pretty little plant quite unlike the other three in appearance, with white-woolly leaves and pink flowers in hop-like clusters.

The marjorams all have a long history of use since classical times, and were more popular in the Middle Ages in Britain than thyme. Culpeper said that 'the oil is very warm and comforting to the joints that are stiff, to mollify and supple them.' Oregano is derived from the Greek *cros*, mountain and *ganos*, joy, beauty, and in Greece it was woven into the crown worn by bridal couples on their wedding day.

Cultivation Sweet marjoram is easily grown, provided the seed is not sown outdoors until the end of late spring, and rigorously protected against frost. Alternatively sow in pots and pot on to grow in 10- or 12cm (4 or 5in) diameter pots. Outdoors, thin to about 20cm (8in) apart, and keep the seedlings clear of weeds. Moist, fertile soil and a sunny, sheltered position are vital. Germination is slow and can take a month in cold soil.

IDENTIFICATION

Height 20cm (8in), spread 15cm (6in)
Root fibrous
Stem angular, tough, woody and brown at the base, otherwise thin and wiry, much branched, light green
Leaf grey-green, soft, oval, entire, 6-20mm (¼-¾in) long, opposite
Flower minute, white to pink, produced from 'knots', green pealike buds formed by closely packed bracts, which are produced in spike-like clusters, June-September; 'knots' elongate with age to resemble catkins
Seed tiny, round, light to dark brown
  Whole plant slightly downy, and spicily and sweetly aromatic

marjoram seeds

USES

Culinary fresh or dried leaves, in meat casseroles shortly before serving, sausages, stuffings, bouquet garni, with mushrooms, egg dishes, cheeses, to flavour vinegar
Medicinal whole flowering plant, fresh or dried, as digestive, or stomachic, as an external antiseptic, once used as ingredient of sneezing powders
Cosmetic for making fragrant soap
Domestic as an insect repellent
Fragrance and Aroma for herb pillows, and tussie mussies

RECIPE

Saucissons Provencal
400g/1 lb pork sausages (without flavouring)
200g/½lb onions
300g/¾lb tomatoes
1 green pepper
salt and pepper
200g/½lb courgettes
1 medium aubergine
1 glass white wine
1 teaspoon chopped fresh marjoram
oil for cooking
Slice the aubergine thickly, salt and leave to sweat. Slice onions, pepper

saucissons provencal

dried marjoram leaves

and courgette, chop tomatoes. Brown sausages quickly in the oil, remove from pan, and sauté the onions without browning. Add peppers and tomatoes and cook for a few minutes, then add the remainder of the vegetables, the marjoram and wine and simmer gently for 30 minutes. Put in a casserole with the sausages and cook in oven at 180°C/350°F/Gas Mark 4 for ¾-1 hour.

wild marjoram

sweet marjoram

MALVACEAE *Althaea officinalis*
Herbaceous perennial

Marshmallow

Hollyhocks are a member of the same family as marshmallow, which has the same large, open saucer-shaped flowers without stems. It seems a more unlikely plant than most to be a herb, but the whole of it, leaves, stems etc., consist of about 30 per cent mucilage, and this has a great number of medicinal applications, known for many centuries. Indeed a mallow was illustrated in a famous herbal of the 6th century A.D., and it may well have been derived from an even earlier Greek herbal of the 2nd century B.C.

Marshmallow has a wide provenance, always found in moist situations, throughout Europe including Britain, Asia, the east of North America and Australia. The sweets called marshmallows do not now contain any of the substance of the plant, being made up of gum, egg-white, flour, sweetening, colouring and so on.

Cultivation Mallows of all kinds are often seen growing on waste ground and beside fields and footpaths, and the marshmallow is no exception, though it favours wet places, especially salt-marshes. It can be started from seed sown outdoors in spring, or by dividing in autumn, as the stems die down, and should be allowed 60cm (2ft) of space from its neighbour. Keep it moist in dry weather.

IDENTIFICATION

Height 1-1.2m (3-4ft), spread 45cm (18in)
Root fleshy, long and tapering, cream-coloured
Stem erect, sparsely branching, green, solid
Leaf ovate-heart-shaped, entire, or 3-5 lobed, the upper leaves narrow at the base rather than heart-shaped, thick, irregularly toothed, shortly stalked, to 7cm (3in) long and 3cm (1¼in) wide
Flower pale pink or white, 5 wedge-shaped petals, toothed at the edge, forming a shallow saucer, singly or in clusters, stamens united into a prominent central tube, darker pink, each flower 3-4cm (1-1¼in) wide, August-September
Seed contained in flat round fruits, turning light brown with maturity, seeds 15-20 in each, also light brown
Whole plant is covered with velvety down, including both leaf surfaces

USES

Culinary young leaves and shoots in salad; roots fried in butter; leaves in soup
Medicinal dried root, two years old, flowers, leaves, for sore throats and mouths, for external and internal ulcers; once used also for sprains, bruises and muscular stiffness
Cosmetic leaves or root in face-packs, root for preventing loss of hair
Domestic not so used
Fragrance and Aroma not present

PRESCRIPTION

Marshmallow milk (for the relief of hoarse coughing and inflammations of the mouth, pharynx and stomach)
25g/1oz/2 tbls grated marshmallow roots
600ml/1 pint/2½ cups milk
1-2 tbls honey according to taste
Put the ingredients in a saucepan and bring slowly to the boil. Then simmer gently for about 30 to 45 minutes.
Take one tablespoon three times a day for hoarse coughs and for the relief of gastric ulcers.

dried marshmallow leaves

marshmallow seeds

marshmallow milk

dried marshmallow root

marshmallow leaves

Mint, Garden

OTHER NAMES: Spearmint

Mint sauce has long been an ingredient of the English Sunday lunch of lamb with the season's new green peas and new potatoes. It is made from *M. spicata*, but there are many other mints with various distinct aromas and flavours – garden mint is the most commonly used and has been so for many centuries. Interestingly, Pliny said of garden mint that 'the smell of Mint does stir up the minde and the taste to a greedy desire of meate'. Introduced to Britain by the Romans and to North America by its first settlers, it has long been used all round the Mediterranean bowl, and continues to be used there today.

The generic and common names of mint are said to be taken from the Greek myth of the nymph Minthe, who was being pursued by Hades, the god of the Underworld. His queen, Persephone, became jealous and turned the nymph into the plant mint.

Its pungent and spicy flavour is unmistakable, and the oil obtained from the plant is that used in the manufacture of spearmint chewing-gum. Although a native of southern Europe, it has become naturalized in the rest of Europe, and is now grown commercially. When buying plants for garden cultivation, it is necessary to be careful to obtain the true garden mint. There is another species called horse mint, *M. longifolia*, which has grey-green leaves, and a very unpleasant smell, quite unlike the true mint, and this often hybridizes with garden mint to produce plants which look like it, but smell completely different. Unfortunately such hybrids are often available as the true mint.

Cultivation There are two problems in growing mint: one is to curtail it, the other is the fungus disease, rust. The plant spreads rapidly by 'runners', the underground root-like stems, and develops shoots at every joint. Some control is obtained by planting it in a bottomless container; spring or autumn are suitable times, and the runners can be detached

IDENTIFICATION

Height 30-45cm (12-18in), spread 15cm (6in) but clumps larger
Root true roots fibrous, but also creeping underground stems, or rhizomes by which plant spreads into clumps
Stem square, green, erect, tough at base, produced from crown and runners
Leaf bright green, almost stalkless, lanceolate, pointed, toothed, opposite, to 6cm (2½in) long
Flower tiny, pale lilac, in clusters on cylindrical spikes to 6cm (2½in) long, August-September
Seed tiny, brown, few

mint julep

ginger mint leaves

black peppermint leaves

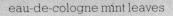

eau-de-cologne mint leaves

and planted, shallowly, to increase it. When flowering stems become apparent they should be removed, to maintain a good supply of leaves. As it dies down in winter, pot-grown plants can be taken under cover in autumn to continue the top growth as long as possible. Symptoms of rust disease are shown as small, reddish-brown, raised spots on the leaf under-surface, and as control is difficult, it is preferable to destroy such plants including the roots, and to plant new specimens in a different place.

Other mints which have similar uses to garden mint include the following. Apple Mint, *M. suaveolens* (syn. *M. rotundifolia*), has a definite and pleasant scent of apples as well as the characteristic mint aroma; the leaves are rounded, toothed and woolly. Eau de Cologne mint is *M. x piperita citrata*, and has a purple tinge to the stems and dark green leaves, and purple runners. It is also known as bergamot, lemon or orange mint, but to the writer, the aroma is definitely that of the famous toilet water.

Ginger mint, *M. x gentilis* 'Variegata', is hotly aromatic, and has yellow variegated, smooth, pointed leaves, the yellow colouring following the veins. Peppermint, *M. x piperita*, needs no description as to smell, but the leaves of black peppermint tend to be ovate, 6cm (2½in) long and 4cm (1½in) wide, and are purple tinged – this is grown commercially and is the one used for peppermint tea, so popular in North Africa. Pineapple mint, *M. rotundifolia* 'Variegata', is a form of the round-leaved mint, which often crosses with *M. longifolia*. Consequently pineapple mint plants tend to vary in the shape of the leaves. However, they always have creamy white variegation at the margins, and sometimes the leaves on one shoot are completely white. They are much wrinkled, long rather than round, and soft with a dull surface. This variety is not quite hardy, particularly in heavy wet soil.

USES

Culinary fresh or dried leaf, in a sauce or jelly to accompany roast meats, and rubbed on to meat before grilling or roasting; with salads, mixed into cheeses, in summer drinks, as part of bouquet garni, and mixed herbs, in chutney
Medicinal fresh or dried leaf; stimulant to appetite, an antiseptic, stomachic, for nervous disorders
Cosmetic fresh leaves, will help heal skin blemishes and act as an astringent, for complexion, use in baths, an ingredient of Hungary water, to flavour toothpaste
Domestic to make aromatic soap and candles
Fragrance and Aroma strongly aromatic leaves, slightly peppermint, hot, contain oil or menthol

RECIPE

Peppermint tisane
1 teaspoon dried peppermint leaves or 2-3 teaspoons fresh whole leaves per person
150ml/¼ pint/⅔ cup water per person
Pour boiling water on to the leaves in a clean container or teapot and leave to stand for 3-10 minutes (no longer, otherwise the flavour changes). Pour through a strainer and serve hot, or iced.

Mint julep
2 measures bourbon whiskey
1 teaspoon castor sugar
sprig of fresh mint
soda to top up
Put the sugar, mint and a little soda into a tall tumbler. Mash these together to release mint flavour. Add the bourbon and then top with soda to taste. Decorate with a sprig of mint.

peppermint tisane

dried peppermint leaves

round-leaved mint

Apple and mint jelly
1 large bunch fresh mint
3 tbls chopped mint
1kg/2lbs cooking apples
600ml/1 pint/2½ cups water
300ml/½ pint/1¼ cups wine vinegar
approx 200g/½lb brown sugar
approx 200g/½lb white sugar
Wash and chop the apples and put
them in a pan with the cold water,
wine vinegar and bunch of mint.
Bring to the boil and simmer for
about 30 minutes or until the apples
are soft. Strain through a jelly bag
overnight. Then measure the juice
and for every 600ml/1 pint/2½ cups
of liquid add 400g/1lb sugar (brown
and white in equal quantities). Boil
to setting point. Leave to cool for
about 10 minutes, then stir in the
chopped mint. Pour into warm,
clean jars and seal when completely
cool.

pineapple mint leaves

spearmint seeds

apple & mint jelly

peppermint leaves

spearmint leaves

ground spearmint leaves

SCROPHULARIACEAE
Verbascum thapsus
Biennial

IDENTIFICATION

Height 2m (6½ft), spread 45cm (18in)
Root tap-root, with fibrous roots
Stem stout, hard beneath a woolly coating of white felt, erect, appears in second season
Leaf large, pointed-oblong, grey-green, thickly white-felted on both sides, in a rosette at the base, and up the stem, to 38cm (15in) long
Flower bright yellow, primrose-like in shape, stalkless, crowded on a spike 30cm (12in) or more long, buds also white-felted, July-September
Seed tiny, many of them, light brown, will self-sow

Mullein

The tall, spire-like stems of this yellow-flowered plant are often seen growing wild in Britain and North America, though it has naturalized itself, and is not indigenous. It is a native of cool temperate climates in Europe and Asia. It is not surprising that it was, and still is, grown as a garden plant, since its large, soft, grey-green leaves and brightly coloured flowers are splendidly ornamental. Perhaps because it has been so popular it has many common names, such as hag taper, Aaron's rod, Adam's flannel and torches.

As well as its medicinal properties, it is associated with magic, and the down on the plant was used by witches to provide wicks for their candles when making incantations and casting spells. One of the 17th-century gardening writers remarked that 'Verbascum is called of the Latines Candela regia . . . because the elder age used the stalks dipped in suet to burne, whether at funeralls or otherwise.'

Cultivation Mullein will always be found growing naturally in well-drained soil and a sunny place. Seed will not germinate in wet heavy soil, and plants that do establish will probably not survive the winter. Allow 60cm (2ft) between plants. Although they are so tall, they will not need staking, and are an excellent plant for a dramatic effect in the garden.

dried mullein flowers

mullein leaves

USES

Culinary not so used
Medicinal fresh leaves, dried leaves or flowers, contain mucilage and used as emollient, in connection with coughs of all kinds including asthmatic, catarrh and other respiratory conditions, mildly sedative
Cosmetic flowers used for lightening hair
Domestic for candle-making, using the stems coated in tallow; down used to supply wicks
Fragrance and Aroma none
Note that the hairs are extremely irritating to the mouth, and any remedies involving mullein should be strained through fine muslin before being taken internally.

RECIPE

Mullein hair rinse (to brighten fair hair)
2 tbls (1 tbls dried) fresh chamomile flowers
2 tbls (1 tbls dried) mullein flowers
2 tbls lemon juice
600ml/1 pint/2½ cups water
Bring the water to the boil, pour over the flowers and leave to infuse for 30 to 60 minutes. Strain, stir in the lemon juice and use as a final hair rinse after shampooing.

mullein seeds

mullein hair rinse

Mustard

Mustard has been used as a flavouring in cooking for thousands of years, and has a worldwide reputation for enhancing a variety of savoury dishes. There are three different kinds of mustard: black mustard, *B. nigra*, discussed here; brown mustard, *B. juncea* and white mustard, *B. alba*; in each case the common name refers to the colour of the seeds. Black mustard is the one with the best and most pungent flavour, and has become naturalized in Britain and America, though it probably originated in the Middle East.

There are references to mustard in Shakespeare: it is the name of one of the fairies in *A Midsummer Night's Dream*, Mustard-seed, and in *Henry IV, Part 2*, Shakespeare refers to 'Tewkesbury mustard', Tewkesbury then being the centre for making it. The Romans soaked the pounded seed in wine and the word mustard is thought to come from the Latin *mustum ardens* meaning 'burning must' – grape must is newly-fermented grape juice. The 16th-century herbalist Gerard recommended that the crushed seed mixed with vinegar was an excellent dish to be eaten with any 'grosse meates'.

Brown mustard is the one grown commercially as it is a shorter plant, at 120-150cm (4-5ft) and the seeds do not fall off easily; it is largely used instead of black mustard, and has a slightly less hot flavour. White mustard seed is mild and is often used as a pickling spice.

English mustard is a yellow powder which is mixed with water and consists of a mixture of black and white mustard seeds. The so-called French mustard is wet, and there are many variations; yellow Dijon is black seed with wine and spices; Bordeaux is dark brown, as it contains the seed husks.

Cultivation Mustard, whether black, brown or white, is grown from seed sown outdoors in spring, and does best in a sunny place and fertile moist soil, when the black mustard is likely to reach its maximum height. Thin the seedlings to 30-45cm (12-18in) apart, and keep free of competing seedlings in the early stages. Seed will be ripe in late summer, and should be watched carefully in the last week or two, or it will easily be lost. It is better to remove the pods before they finish maturing, and allow the seeds to ripen in the pods.

USES

Culinary crushed seed supplies a hot flavour to enhance the taste of any savoury dish, such as roast or cold meats, sausages; used in sauces and dressings, with cooked cheese dishes; seedlings used as salad in mustard and cress, or as part of sprouting seeds

Medicinal seed, leaves; add ground seed to hot water as foot-bath; use mustard flour as soothing poultice for chilblains; as an emetic, a tablespoonful of mustard flour in luke-warm water

Cosmetic none

Domestic none

Fragrance and Aroma none

RECIPE

Celery pickle with mustard seeds

400g/1lb celery
2 green peppers
1 red pepper
1 yellow pepper
4 teaspoons mustard seeds
200g/8oz/1 cup sugar
4 teaspoons salt
1 teaspoon ground tumeric
600ml/1 pint/2½ cups white malt vinegar
2 tbls cornflour

Slice the celery and onions, core, seed and dice the peppers. Cover the vegetables with boiling water in a bowl. Leave for about 15 minutes before draining. Put the mustard seeds, sugar, salt, tumeric and vinegar in a saucepan and bring to the boil. Add the drained vegetables and cook for a further 5 minutes, stirring all the time. Add the cornflour blended with ½ cup of water and cook for another 5 minutes. Pour into hot, sterilized preserving jars and seal.

IDENTIFICATION

Height 1-3 metres (3½-10ft), spread 30cm (12in)

Root white, fibrous and with central short anchor root

Stem grey-green, smooth, much branched

Leaf grey-green, stalked, lower ones large to 15cm (6in), bristly, lobed, upper on stem narrow, pointed, entire

Flower yellow, 4-petalled, rounded, 1.5cm (½in) wide, in long clusters, early-late summer

Seed dark brown to black, rounded, contained in long narrow, flattened pods with a short beak, close against the stem

black mustard seeds

brown mustard seeds

celery pickle with mustard seeds

mustard seedlings

mustard & cress

URTICACEAE *Urtica dioica*
Herbaceous perennial

Nettle

The old story about the Roman legionaries using nettles to keep themselves warm on night duty in the cold northern province that was Britain may be apocryphal, but there is no doubt that the sting resulting from the touch of a nettle leaf causes a burning sensation. This is because each hair consists of a sharp, hollow spine, the walls of which contain silica, making them glass-like and brittle. The point of the spine breaks off easily, and the liquid inside, formic acid, is released into the object causing the injury, in most cases the skin of an animal.

In spite of this anti-social habit, nettles are of considerable use in many ways, including culinary; they contain vitamins A and C and, it is said, more iron than spinach, together with a variety of other minerals.

Cultivation The discouragement of nettles, rather than their encouragement, is usually the object of many gardeners, but for those who need to grow them, loose, fertile soil with plenty of nitrogen in it, and a little shade will produce the tallest plants. Plants will self-sow, as well as spreading by underground stems. A variety of insects including butterfly and moth caterpillars feed on them.

IDENTIFICATION

Height to 1.8m (6ft), but usually 60-90cm (2-3ft), spread 23cm (9in)
Root yellow, tough, branching and spreading widely
Stem erect, bristly, dull green; some also spreading shallowly underground as rhizomes to produce new patches of plant some distance from the parent
Leaf green, sharply toothed, pointed-heart-shaped, to 12cm (5in), long, hairy, opposite, stalked
Flower minute, greenish, in dangling catkin-like clusters, June-September
Seed yellowish-grey, tiny

USES

Culinary young fresh leaves and stems, as spinach alternative, added to casseroles, to make cheese, and nettle beer
Medicinal fresh or dried leaves for rheumatism, to control internal bleeding, for many skin problems, a good diuretic
Cosmetic to prevent dandruff, and to tone the skin and improve the circulation, using leaves in infusion or decoction; use juice to encourage hair growth
Domestic roots provide a dye, grey, yellow or orangey depending on mordant; fresh leaves as a liquid fertilizer, compost accelerator, and insecticide; fibre of roots once widely used for making cloth, twine; fresh leaves as fly deterrent
Fragrance and Aroma slightly aromatic

PRESCRIPTION

Nettle soup (for anaemia; also mildly laxative)
The common and despised nettle contains a high proportion of vitamins and minerals and other active substances which give it wide therapeutic application. Its iron content is of great value to those with anaemia, while the powdered leaf is used as a snuff which rapidly halts nose bleeds in those suffering from weakened blood vessels in the nose.
400g/¹/₂lb young nettle tops
50g/2oz/¹/₄ cup butter
900ml/1¹/₂ pints/3³/₄ cups milk
salt and pepper to taste
Melt the butter in a saucepan, add the nettles and stew gently for about 10 minutes. Add the milk, bring to the boil and simmer for a further 10 minutes. Allow the soup to cool slightly, then purée in a blender.

dried nettle leaves

nettle soup

nettle leaves & flowers

Return the soup to a clean pan, add salt and pepper to taste and reheat. (For a more substantial soup, add 2 or 3 parboiled potatoes at the same time as the milk and simmer until they are soft before puréeing the mixture.)

Orris Root

The iris is one of the longest-cultivated flowering plants, and one variety, thought to be this one, can be recognized on the wall of an Egyptian temple at Karnak dating from 1500 B.C.

These beautiful and delicate flowers, often heavily scented, include the complete range of colour as we know it, hence the name, which is the Greek word for rainbow, and from which the word 'orris' is directly derived. The violet-scented root or rhizome of the plant is of prime importance in perfumery, though that of other iris species such as *germanica* itself and *pallida* are also fragrant. Its production has become associated with Italy, and in particular the Florence area, where it is represented in the heraldic arms of that city. It is also said to be the *fleur-de-lis* of French heraldry.

From southern Europe, and naturalized in Iran, northern India and similar areas, orris root was once used medicinally as a purgative. It is now considered too strong for internal use and can cause vomiting. It grows well throughout North America except in the warm moist climate of Florida and the Gulf Coast.

Cultivation As with most irises, the Florentine iris needs plenty of sun, and a dry, well-drained soil. Planting should be in April, and the best plants will be obtained in soil which is deep and fertile. The rhizomes can be divided in late spring, to flower the following summer, and each should have a bud or shoot on it. The divisions are planted so that half the rhizome is above the soil surface, as they rot if covered with soil. They need to be divided every few years, so that good flowers will continue to appear. The rhizomes should be dug up in autumn and dried immediately, but the full violet fragrance will not be apparent until the roots are two years old.

USES

Culinary not so used
Medicinal not now used
Cosmetic dried root, powdered, used as part of mixture for dry shampoo; to make bath salts, perfumed talcum powder
Domestic in herb pillows, to perfume household linen and clothing
Fragrance and Aroma dried root strongly violet-scented increasing with age; used as fixative in potpourri, in perfumery manufacture, as part of 'frangipani', the Italian perfume named after the tropical tree whose flowers have the same fragrance

RECIPE

Dry Elizabethan potpourri
10 parts dried damask rose petals and rose geranium leaves, well mixed
5 parts dried lavender flowers and sweet marjoram leaves
⅛ part each powdered cloves, cinnamon, nutmeg, allspice, mace
⅓ part each powdered orris root and ground gum benzoin
20 drops rose geranium oil
5 drops sandalwood oil
Blend the spices with the petals, lavender and leaves; add the spices, fixatives and oils, stir regularly everyday for a week, longer if possible, keeping closed, and then transfer to bowls.

IRIDACEAE *Iris germanica florentina*
Herbaceous perennial

IDENTIFICATION

Height 60-90cm (2-3ft), spread 15cm (6in), but increases yearly
Root true roots small and fibrous, main 'root' a stout fleshy rhizome, white internally
Stem green, erect, stout, fleshy, sheathed in leaves, 60-90cm (2-3ft) tall
Leaf green, sword-shaped, 45cm long, 2.5-3cm (1-1¼in) wide
Flower white, tinted pale violet, with yellow beard, or pure white with no beard, 6-7.5cm (2½-3in) long, June-July, unscented
Seed round, light brown

orris root & leaves

dried orris root

Elizabethan potpourri

| UMBELLIFERAE
Petroselinum crispum
Biennial/short-lived
perennial

Parsley

This herb needs no introduction to European and North American readers; indeed it is one of the oldest and longest-used herbs known to man. It was described in a Greek herbal written in the third century B.C. and is probably a native of the eastern Mediterranean area, though it is now so widespread it is difficult to be certain of its origin.

Pliny described it as being of use, if scattered in a pool, for curing unhealthy fish; it was said to have been grown in the Emperor Charlemagne's herb garden; Ion the Gardener who wrote the first book about gardening in Britain included it as his favourite herb, and it was mentioned in Langland's famous poem *Piers Plowman*. So its recorded history progresses without a break to the present time, mainly as a culinary herb, but also having some medicinal value, as well as cosmetic and domestic use.

Cultivation Parsley is hardy and can be sown outdoors in March, but takes several weeks to germinate if sown at that time in cool temperate regions, hence it has earnt itself the reputation of needing 'to go to the Devil seven times and back' before it will sprout. However, if sown later in the spring when the soil is warm, it will germinate within two weeks or less. Sown in early July, it is up in a matter of days. The traditional short-cut of pouring boiling water into the seed-drill acknowledges its need for warmth.

Parsley should have a deep, moist fertile soil for ideal growth, and sun or a little shade. Seedlings should be sown where they are to grow and thinned twice to a final spacing of 20cm (8in); good plants occupy a square foot of space. By the same token, parsley in pots should have a good potting compost, No 2 if John Innes is used (see page 36 for recipe), and at least a 12cm (5in) diameter pot, 15cm (6in) if possible, to provide depth for the tap-root and sufficient food and moisture.

Spring-sown parsley will provide leaves in winter, but a better supply will be provided with early July-sown plants, covering both with cloches or tunnels if snow is likely. In the second summer, when flowers appear, allow them to self-seed.

IDENTIFICATION

Height flowering stem average 30-45cm (12-18in), spread 23cm (9in)
Root tap-root, white, like small carrot
Stem green, solid, erect
Leaf green, pinnate, leaflets so much curled that pinnate quality is not apparent, each leaflet section up to 2.5cm (1in) long, forms basal cluster in first year
Flower tiny, yellow-green in umbellifer clusters, July-September of 2nd year
Seed tiny, black

dried parsley leaves

parsley seeds

parsley leaves

bouquet garni

fines herbes

USES

Culinary fresh (preferably) or dried leaf, for sauces, as garnish for salads, vegetables, potatoes, as part of bouquet garni, with egg dishes, for omelette *fines herbes*, soup, marinades, in casseroles added at start and near end of cooking
Medicinal fresh or dried leaf, dried root, dried seed; contains vitamin C; as a tonic and stomachic, for flatulence, a diuretic and of considerable help in many kidney complaints
Cosmetic to prevent thread veins in the complexion; said to remove freckles
Domestic as a dye, to provide cream or shades of green depending on mordant
Fragrance and Aroma leaves and stems strongly aromatic, roots less so

RECIPE

Bouquet garni
2 sprigs parsley
2 springs thyme
1 bay leaf
Tie in a bundle and add to casseroles, stews and sauces. For pork, substitute sage for the bay leaf.

Bouquet garni for fish
2 sprigs of parsley
1 sprig tarragon
1 dry fennel stalk
1 leaf lemon balm
Tie in a bundle and add to the cooking liquid.

Fines herbes
A classic addition to omelettes
1 part parsley
1 part chervil
½ part chives
1-2 leaves tarragon
Chop herbs finely and add to omelettes and other egg dishes.

Pennyroyal

IDENTIFICATION

Height prostrate, wide-spreading to 30cm (12in)
Root fibrous, shallow
Stem green, weakly creeping along soil, rooting at leaf-joints, square; flowering stems to 20cm (8in)
Leaf dark green, oval, roundly or sharply toothed, slightly downy, 6-12mm (¼-½in) long, 6mm (¼in) wide, shortly stalked, opposite
Flower red-purple to mauve, tiny, in dense rounded clusters in tiers up the stems, July-August
Seed light brown, minute, oval

Although this is a species of mint, it is dealt with separately, as it is so unlike other mints in growth habit. It is flat and mat-like, because the prostrate stems root as they lengthen. It has a stronger aroma and hotter flavour than its relations, not always to everyone's liking but, provided it is used taking this into account, it is one of the best culinary herbs. It is a native of Europe, Asia and North Africa, now naturalized in North and South America.

It is certainly amongst the oldest of the European herbs, and it was its very pungency that made it popular with the palates of our tougher ancestors. There are frequent references to it in Anglo-Saxon writings, and the Greeks and Romans made much use of it; the Greek army doctor Dioscorides listed it amongst medical herbs, and Pliny also describes it. Its common name derives from 'pulioll-royall', an old French name for a royal thyme. *Pulegium* is from *pulex*, the Latin for flea, as it was much used to deter, if not actually kill, fleas. Two varieties have been distinguished, *M. p. decumbens*, the one under discussion, and *M. p. erecta*, whose flower stems are 20-30cm (8-12in) tall. The North American pennyroyal (*Hedeoma pulgeogioides*) is a quite different plant but with many of the same characteristics as *Mentha pulegium*; it has a strong minty smell and in Indian folk medicine was used as an intestinal irritant and an abortion-causing agent, as well as an insect repellent.

Cultivation English pennyroyal needs a moist soil. In the wild it is usually found growing beside streams and ponds. It also needs fertility, but is indifferent to sun or light shade. Planting can be in autumn or spring, the latter if winters are likely to be severe. Space the plants 15cm (6in) apart each way, and always keep moist in dry weather. It will also grow from seed sown in late spring, with protection, planting out about six weeks later. It is one of the aromatic alternatives to grass for a lawn, being mown twice a year only, and will also grow from cracks in paving.

USES

Culinary fresh or dried leaves, use sparingly in same way as other mints (see p. 86)
Medicinal fresh or dried flowering plant, for colds, headache, nausea, flatulence; should not be used where kidney disease present or in pregnancy; to relieve pain of insect bites and stings and ward off biting insects
Cosmetic use in water for washing
Domestic for strewing, to repel fleas, ants and flies, in household linen and clothing

RECIPE

Pennyroyal dumplings
Serve with a well-flavoured lamb or beef stew
100g/4oz/1 cup self-raising flour
50g/2oz/¼ cup suet
1 tbls chopped pennyroyal leaves
water
Combine the ingredients with enough water to make a doughy but not sticky consistency and form into balls about 2.5cm (1in) in diameter. Add to a moist beef or lamb stew about half-an-hour before the end of the cooking time, making sure there is enough liquid in which the dumplings can cook.

pennyroyal dumplings

erect pennyroyal leaves

creeping pennyroyal

Pink

Also called the clove pink, clove July or carnation in modern times, this species was once widely known as the gillyflower, derived eventually from the Arabic *quaranful*, a clove, by way of the Greek *karyophillon*, the Latin *caryophyllus*, the Italian *garofolo* and the French *giroflée*. Its strong, sweet, clove-like scent has made it popular both for culinary and perfumery purposes for more than 2,000 years. In the first century A.D. Pliny wrote that it was discovered in Spain in the previous century, where it was used to spice drinks, and in England in mediaeval times it was known as 'sops-in-wine', being mixed with wine and ale as a substitute for the costly cloves from the Far East.

It grows wild in southern Europe and India and has become naturalized elsewhere in Europe, including England, where it has been found growing literally out of castle walls, notably the Norman ones.

Cultivation The true clove-pink, being wild, needs no special cultivation, provided it has a truly well-drained soil, short of plant nutrient, and a sunny sheltered site. It can be increased by layering in August, or by division at the same time. Seed is also possible, in mid to late spring. It varies considerably in the wild, where doubled flowers and differences in height, colour, habit and shape of petal all occur frequently. This tendency to vary has been exploited in the breeding of the modern hybrid border carnation, an example of which is shown here.

USES

Culinary fresh flowers, to flavour jams, syrups, sauces, vinegar, jellies, butter, wine, cordials, decorate salads and soups
Medicinal not so used now, though once used to cover up the flavour of unpleasant medicines
Cosmetic used in home-made colognes
Domestic used as an ingredient for snuff, to perfume clothing and household linen
Fragrance and Aroma strongly clove-scented; used as substitute for cloves; in potpourri, tussie-mussies, herb pillows

RECIPE

Syrup of pinks
400g/1lb flower petals
1 litre/2 pints/5 cups water
12 cloves
400g/1lb sugar
Put the petals, cloves and water into a heatproof jar and cover tightly with kitchen foil and a lid. Place the jar in a saucepan of cold water so that the jar is about ¾ covered by water. Bring slowly to the boil and simmer for 5-6 hours topping up the saucepan with boiling water from time to time. Drain the contents of the jar into a bowl and squeeze all moisture from the petals before discarding them. Measure the liquid from the jar and for each 600ml/1 pint/2½ cups, add 400g/1lb of sugar. Boil again until the sugar melts and the mixture is a syrup. Leave to cool, then bottle and secure tightly.

CARYOPHYLLACEAE
Dianthus caryophyllus
Herbaceous perennial

IDENTIFICATION

Height 45-60cm (18-24in), spread 30cm (12in)
Root fibrous, spreading
Stem grey-green, thick leaf-joints, erect, slender, hard
Leaf grey-green, long, narrow and pointed, 7-12cm (3-5in) long, 6mm (¼in) wide, opposite, keeled
Flower rose-pink, or purple-red, 2.5cm (1in) wide, solitary or in clusters of up to 6, with 5 petals fringed at the edges, strongly fragrant, July
Seed tiny, black

pink flowers & stems

syrup of pink ingredients

Rose

There are several other species of roses with herbal connotations, such as *R. canina, rubiginosa, rugosa, centifolia, damascena* and *indica*, but this, the apothecary's rose, sometimes known as the red damask rose, because it was thought to have been introduced from Damascus by a Crusader, had the greatest medicinal use. In general, roses have played a part in everyday life from the time of the ancient Egyptians and Chinese, and have always been loved and treated with veneration, and repeatedly illustrated in herbals and paintings; they were adopted as the national flower in Britain from the Middle Ages. The damask rose is extremely fragrant and one of the sources of attar (oil) of roses; others are *R. centifolia*, the cabbage rose, and *R. indica*, the tea rose. The apothecary's rose grows at Provins in France and has the property that it keeps its perfume even when the petals have been dried and powered, thus making it of great use to add to medicinal compounds and ensuring that they are pleasant and soothing.

Cultivation The apothecary's rose is hardy and will do well in deep, well-drained but moist soil, in sun or a little shade at some time during the day. Plant between autumn and spring, and be careful to spread the roots down and out round the plant, so that they are not forced into an unnatural position. Little pruning is needed, but if necessary do it in early spring, so as to remove dead growth, and straggling and weak shoots; thin any which are crowded. Remove the flowers as they fade. Pests and disease are unlikely to attack. Mulch in late spring with rotted organic matter, and give a light dressing of bonfire ash in spring, or any fertilizer which contains potassium, if flowering is poor.

IDENTIFICATION

Height 60-90cm (2-3ft), spread similar
Root tough, woody, deeply penetrating, brown skin, white internally, also fibrous
Stem brown and woody to green and firm, erect, branching, prickly
Leaf green, three-five leaflets, each ovate, toothed, deeply veined
Flower pink to deep crimson, semi-double, 3.5-7cm (1½-3in) wide, June, July
Seed small, roundish, biscuit colour, contained in brick red hips

rugosa rose hips

rose petal jam

rose hip tea

rose petals

Rue

Rue, although it is strongly flavoured, has a most bitter and acrid taste, which makes it unpopular for culinary use now, except in one or two specialized cases. It was never greatly used in food, even in mediaeval times, but it had considerable medicinal application, and still has, for certain ailments. However, it has to be so used with great care, and preferably only by trained and professional medical advisers.

Its native habitat is southern Europe, where it grows on rocky hill and mountainsides, from the most inhospitable soil. The plant was prescribed by the ancient Greeks to improve eyesight and this belief continued and travelled to Britain where Gerard recommended: 'that the herb a little boiled or skalded and kept in pickle as Sampier (samphire) and eaten, quickens the sight', or: 'applied with honey and the juice of Fennell, is a remedie against dim eies'. The name is taken from the Greek *reuo*, to set free, because it was thought to be effective in so many ailments.

Cultivation The species described is a pretty, small shrub, the leaves of which are the most decorative part. It can be clipped to formal shapes so that the flowers are prevented from developing, the plant thus being covered in the delicate, lace-like foliage. There is a cultivar 'Jackman's Blue', whose leaves are distinctly blue, and this is even more striking. Rue needs poor, dry soil and plenty of sun and warmth to flourish and ripen its seed. Planting should be in spring, when seed may also be sown – it germinates easily – or semi-hardwood cuttings can be made in summer, and rooted under cover.

USES

Culinary fresh or dried leaf, sparingly, in salads, sandwiches, with cheeses, and to flavour beer
Medicinal leaf, fresh or dried, to treat skin disorders, as an eye lotion, a gargle, for rheumatism, traditionally used for epilepsy, an abortifacient, toxic in large amounts
Cosmetic not so used
Domestic powerful flea repellent, also against other insects, as an air cleanser when burnt
Fragrance and Aroma bitterly aromatic, unpleasantly so; oil is used in perfumery

PRESCRIPTION

Rue eyewash
Rue is an example of a common, well-known garden herb, with a long history of use, yet with properties that make it unsuitable for general use by the layman. Its complicated chemical structure includes bergaptens, which may cause an allergic rash on the hands of those using it, and other substances which strictly *prohibit* its intake by pregnant women. The substance rutin strengthens weakened blood vessels, particularly in the eye.

As such it has been used as a very weak tea (6g/¼oz to 600ml/1 pint/2½ cups of water) (one cup per day) by male artists and craftsmen. Today the herb tea should only be used as an external eye wash. Prepare the above tea and dilute 1:10 with clean, sterile water and use an eye bath.

IDENTIFICATION

Height 45-60cm (18-24in), spread 20-30cm (8-12in)
Root tough, fibrous, some fleshy anchoring roots, white
Stem green, brown and woody when mature, erect, branching
Leaf blue-green, thin, deeply divided, leaf sections oblong with rounded ends, semi-evergreen, alternate, to 1.5cm (½in) long
Flower yellow, four petals, 1.2cm (½in) wide, in loose clusters, June-September
Seed tiny, black

chopped rue

rue eyewash

rue leaves & flower buds

LABIATAE Salvia officinalis
Evergreen Sub-shrub

Sage

The use of sage, whether for medicinal or culinary purposes, dates back in Europe at least several centuries B.C., when it was listed in Theophrastus' writings on plants. The Romans made much use of it also, its generic name being derived from *salvere*, to be well, and in the Middle Ages, there was a current Arabic saying: 'Why should a man die when there is sage in his garden?' It was considered particularly helpful in soothing and calming the nervous and hysterical.

Its original home was Spain and western Yugoslavia, but it has spread widely round the Mediterranean coastline, particularly where the soil is well-drained and alkaline, with plenty of sun. The highly aromatic leaves have many uses, and also make it a decorative garden shrub; there are several varieties with leaves of other colours besides green.

Cultivation Sage can be grown outdoors in cool, temperate climates in spite of its provenance, and will survive all but the coldest winters, provided the soil is well-drained, and the plant has been well-ripened as a result of growing in a sunny position. Plant in spring and take tip cuttings in summer, to root under cover; sage can also be layered in spring. It will need renewing every seven years or so as it is not long-lived. Prune by cutting off the old flowered growth immediately after flowering, when it will produce good new shoots. *S. o.* 'Purpurascens' has violet-tinted leaves; 'Icterina' has leaves variegated with yellow, and 'Tricolor' has foliage veined with creamy white and pink, becoming red.

IDENTIFICATION

Height 30-75cm (1-2½ft) tall, and as much wide
Root fibrous, wide-spreading
Stem tough, brown and woody at the base, new stems, square, green, soft, much branched
Leaf light grey-green, oblong with rounded tips, much wrinkled, soft on upper surface, 3-5.6cm (1¼-2¼in) long, opposite
Flower bright blue-purple, two-lipped tubular, about 2.5cm (1in) long, in clusters spaced along the end part of a shoot to form a spike-like inflorescence, June-July
Seed tiny, black

USES

Culinary fresh or dried leaves, with rich and fatty meats of all kind including game, in stuffings, marinades, with salads, sausages, cheeses, fish particularly oily kinds, bouquet garni
Medicinal leaves, fresh or dried, oil; an antiseptic and astringent, for sore throats, to treat skin troubles, ulcerated mouth, of help with quinsy and tonsillitis, as a soothing and calming drink
Cosmetic to darken and improve the colour of hair, and to increase its growth, to whiten teeth, and strengthen gums, an astringent and deodorant, for bath and washing water
Domestic for strewing, flowers once used to dye food
Fragrance and Aroma leaves strongly and penetratingly aromatic, flavour somewhat bitter

RECIPE

Sage and onion sauce
(for roast pork, goose or duck)
This 17th century recipe is a variation on the now more common sage and onion stuffing.
1 medium onion chopped finely
2 tablespoons chopped sage
25g/1oz/1½ cup fine breadcrumbs
25g/1oz/2 tbls butter
150ml/¼ pint/⅔ cup well-flavoured roast juices, or gravy
salt and pepper to taste
Gently cook the onion and sage in the butter for about 10 minutes or until the onion is soft (do not allow to brown). Then add the breadcrumbs and the roast juices or gravy. Cook for a few minutes more, stirring thoroughly. Add salt and pepper to taste before serving.

sage & onion sauce

chopped sage leaves

dried sage leaves

sage leaves

sage seeds

LABIATAE *Satureja* spp
Tender annual,
sub-shrub

Savory

IDENTIFICATION

S. hortensis
Root fibrous, shallow
Height 30cm (12in) spread 15cm (6in)
Stem square, dark green, erect, branching
Leaf dark green, narrow, entire, 1.2-2.5cm (½-1in) long, 2mm (⅛in) wide, opposite
Flower pale lilac-mauve, small, two-lipped tubular, long-lasting July-October
Seed round, dark brown to black, tiny

S. montana
Root fibrous, and a dark brown tap root
Height to 38cm (15in) spread 20cm (8in)
Stem brown and woody at base, young stems green and square; branching, bushy
Leaf grey-green, shiny, more pointed, slightly larger, otherwise similar
Flower white or pink, appearing in more spike-like clusters, otherwise similar
Seed similar

The savories are not as well known as the majority of culinary herbs, but they should be used as often as marjoram or basil are, as they have their own distinctive, spicy, warming flavour to add to many dishes. Traditionally they are associated with all kinds of bean dishes, and are good digestants in that they prevent flatulence.

Summer savory planted in patches is highly ornamental in flower, being covered with small, light purple flowers for many weeks, and accordingly festooned with bees with which it is very popular.

Savory has a longer history than sage, though not considered to be as useful medicinally. Its stimulant effect may account for its reputation as an aphrodisiac, its generic name being thought to come from satyr. *S. hortensis* (summer savory) is the annual; *S. montana* (winter savory) a perennial shrub, whose leaves have a stronger, but less pleasant flavour. However, it is a hardy plant.

Cultivation Summer savory is grown as a half-hardy annual, sowing outdoors in April-May, to thin to 20cm (8in) apart, when the plants will grow into little bushes, but be killed by the first hard frost in autumn. Winter savory can be grown from seed sown outdoors in August; it should *not* be covered as it needs light to germinate when it will then sprout in about ten days. Grow at the same spacing. It can also be increased by layering, from soft cuttings or division in early spring, and grows for many years. Both kinds thrive with good drainage, rather poor soil, and plenty of sun.

USES

Culinary fresh or dried leaves, with beans of all kinds, in stuffings, with any kind of pork meat, with game, in bean or lentil soups, wherever a warm-hot flavour is required
Medicinal leaves fresh or dried, dried flowering tops, a tonic, digestive, antiseptic and diuretic; said to relieve pain of wasp and bee stings at once
Cosmetic not so used
Domestic for strewing
Fragrance and Aroma leaves hot, slightly peppery in aroma and flavour; winter savory strongest

RECIPE

Broad beans with savory and ham
200g/½lb young shelled broad beans
50g/2oz/¼ cup butter
1 teaspoon chopped, fresh summer savory
1 thick slice of ham
boiling water
Melt half the butter in a saucepan, add the beans and cook gently for a couple of minutes, stirring, then add the savory and just enough boiling water to cover the beans. Boil rapidly for about 5-10 minutes until the beans are tender and the liquid almost evaporated. Chop up the ham and add to the beans with the remaining butter. Add salt and pepper to taste and serve.

summer savory seeds

winter savory leaves

dried summer savory leaves

summer savory

broad beans with savory & ham

Sorrel

OTHER NAMES: Buckler-leaved sorrel

There are two sorts of sorrel commonly grown as herbs: the English and the French. The former has large, long, pointed bright green leaves, the latter has rounded, much smaller leaves, with a much better flavour, and it is this which is used by the French for making soup.

Sorrels in general were used by the Greeks and Romans for medicinal purposes, and had some medicinal as well as culinary application in mediaeval Britain, but the English sorrel then used (*R. acetosa*) was replaced for culinary purposes by the French version and has been so used until the present day. Its sour but refreshing flavour, due to the presence of oxalic acid, is particularly agreeable in salads for which fresh, young leaves should be used. It is native to Europe and Asia, growing mainly in well-drained ground on hill and mountainsides, and wasteland; it is naturalized in a few places in Britain and grows well in temperate to warm regions of North America.

Cultivation French sorrel grows easily from seed sown outdoors in mid-spring, when it may also be planted. Sun or a little shade and a moist but well-drained soil are preferable, allowing plants 45cm (18in) between them. To ensure as much foliage as possible, flowering stems should be removed as they appear. It will grow in alkaline soil, but does better in an acid one.

USES

Culinary fresh leaves, for soups, salads, with rich or fatty meat dishes, in stuffings for fish dishes, for sauces, in omelettes as a substitute for spinach
Medicinal no regular medicinal use, but leaves have diuretic effects
Cosmetic not so used
Domestic not so used
Fragrance and Aroma bruised leaves have strong aroma and taste refreshingly astringent

RECIPE

A variation of the traditional French sorrel soup.
Sorrel and tomato soup
200g/½lb fresh, finely chopped sorrel leaves
100g/¼lb peeled and chopped tomatoes
900ml/1½ pints/3¾ cups chicken stock
25g/1oz/2 tbls butter
salt, pepper and sugar to taste
Sauté sorrel in butter briefly until wilted. Add the tomatoes and cook for about 5 minutes until they are soft but not completely disintegrated. Heat the stock, add to sorrel and tomatoes with salt, pepper and a little sugar to taste. Bring to the boil and simmer for about 5 minutes before serving.

POLYGONACEAE *Rumex scutatus*
Herbaceous perennial

IDENTIFICATION

Height 15cm (6in), but flowering stems to 30cm (12in), spread 23cm (9in)
Root fleshy but thin, tapering and widespreading, a few fibrous
Stem light green, sprawling, branching, somewhat succulent
Leaf grey-green, thick, almost fleshy, rounded shield-shaped, up to 3cm (1½in) long and as much wide
Flower tiny, greenish, in loose spikes early-mid summer
Seed tiny, brown

English sorrel

sorrel seeds

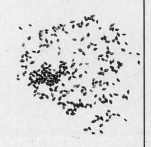

French sorrel

sorrel & tomato soup

Southernwood

OTHER NAMES: Lad's love

If bees are to be encouraged in the garden, this is not a plant to grow, as it is said to be a strong repellent to them, and also to other insects; this gave it the name of *garderobe* by the French, when it was placed in wardrobes to prevent moth infestation.

The filigree fineness of its leaves help it to be one of the most attractive of small garden shrubs. In fact Dioscorides described it as having 'very small leaves as if it were seen rather as furnished with hair'.

The name 'lad's love' came from the practice of its ashes being made into a paste and then rubbed on the face to hasten beard growth, and in his *Herbal*, Culpeper recommends that 'the ashes mingled with old salad oil, helps those that are bald, causing the hair to grow again on the head or beard'.

Cultivation Southernwood is a pretty garden plant, lending a delicate airiness to a border, especially appropriate to a collection of grey and silver plants, and helping to create that marvellous mixture of aromas and fragrances so often met with on the sunny hillsides of the Mediterranean. It is not evergreen. Plant in spring, and allow about 60cm (2ft) between plants; light sandy soil containing well-rotted organic matter and a sunny place will keep it long-lived, though severe winters may damage it. It is increased by soft cuttings of new shoots in summer, kept under cover until rooted. Pruning or clipping is only necessary if it becomes lax or poorly leafed, then cut it back in mid-late spring moderately hard.

IDENTIFICATION

Height 60-90cm (2-3ft), spread 45-75cm (1½-2½ft)
Root fibrous, widespreading
Stem erect, brown and woody at base, much branched to form small shrub, young shoots green and soft, round
Leaf grey-green, very finely divided to produce a filmy, feathery effect, each complete leaf 5-7cm (2-3in) long, alternate
Flower dull yellow, tiny, 4mm (⅙in) wide, in loose clusters, often not produced in cool temperate climates, otherwise August-September
Seed minute, brown

USES

Culinary fresh or dried leaves occasionally used in Europe as part of stuffing for poultry
Medicinal whole plant, dried, is a stimulant, antiseptic, a vermifuge, once mixed with treacle when treating children
Cosmetic the leaves as an infusion mixed with Eau-de-Cologne to encourage hair growth and check dandruff
Domestic repels moth, flea and other insects from household linen, clothing and carpeting; stems will supply a deep yellow dye
Fragrance and Aroma: highly and sweetly aromatic, refreshing and reviving, used in potpourri

HOUSEHOLD USE

Southernwood coat hanger herb bag (insect repellent)
1 heaped tbls dried southernwood
1 teaspoon crushed cinnamon stick
Muslin bag, triangular, each side 5cm/2in long
Crumble the dried southernwood and mix with the crushed cinammon. Fill the muslin bag with herbs and attach to the coathanger with a ribbon. A very effective moth repellent for winter suits and coats when in store over the summer months.

southernwood herb bag

southernwood leaves & stem

dried southernwood leaves

Sweet Cicely

A little known herb with a delightful name, sweet cicely looks like a more delicate version of cow parsley, another umbellifer, but the aniseed scent of its leaves gives it away; the roots have the same smell. It is a handsome plant and, although large, grows neatly and tidily without needing support, and so lends itself well to a herbaceous border. As a native of Europe including Britain, there is no difficulty in cultivation. It grows well in temperate to warm regions in North America.

The Greek name is thought to be an allusion to the aroma of its leaves which is reminiscent of myrrh; the prefix 'sweet' indicates their flavour and the use to which they can be put. In Gerard's time and later when Culpeper wrote his *Herbal*, it was called sweet chervil as well. Gerard remarked that 'the seeds eaten as a salad whiles they are yet with oile, vinegar and pepper exceed all other salads'.

Cultivation The choice of site for sweet cicely should be carefully made, as digging up a mature plant is a long hard job, especially as it is important to remove all the roots. One of the methods of increase is to chop the roots into sections, on each of which there is an eye, and replant them 5cm (2in) deep in spring. It will also self-seed, provided the soil is acid, but is slow to germinate as it needs a period of cold first. A deep moist soil is important; a little shade is preferable. The leaves start to appear in February and may still be present in December, which makes it particularly useful, since the dried leaves do not retain their aroma well. The tiny white flowers are bee-attractants.

USES

Culinary fresh leaves, seed, root; leaves to replace sugar in tart fruit dishes, chopped and added to fruit salads, in vegetable salads, herb butter, boiled roots with oil and lemon, chopped green seeds also for flavouring, used in Chartreuse liqueur
Medicinal not so used at present, though leaves can be used by diabetics to replace sugar
Cosmetic not so used
Domestic chopped seeds which are rich in oil, once used to perfume furniture polish
Fragrance and Aroma leaves, roots and seeds strong sweet aroma and taste of aniseed

RECIPE

Summer fruit salad with sweet cicely
2 peaches
1 small melon
2 plums
100g/4oz/¼lb seedless grapes
100g/4oz/¼lb strawberries
juice of 2 oranges
juice of ½ lemon
1-2 tbls caster sugar
1½ tbls chopped sweet cicely
Skin and stone peaches, wash and stone plums, peel the grapes. Chop all fruit into small pieces, add the orange, lemon juice and sugar according to sweetness desired. Stir in the chopped sweet cicely and serve in a glass bowl.

UMBELLIFERAE *Myrrhis odorata*
Herbaceous perennial

IDENTIFICATION

Height after several years, 1.5m (5ft), spread 90cm (3ft)
Root many, thick, fleshy, pale brown outside, white inside, deeply and tenaciously penetrating
Stem green, erect, stout, hollow, ridged, branching
Leaf light green above, very pale beneath, delicately fern-like, up to 30cm (12in) long, two-three pinnate, each segment toothed, oblong
Flower white, tiny, in umbel clusters up to 5cm (2in) wide, bracts finely fringed, whitish, late spring-early summer
Seed brown to black, long and narrow, to 2.5cm (1in), ridged

sweet cicely leaves

sweet cicely seeds

sweet cicely fruit salad

Tansy

Somehow tansy seems to be very much a herb associated with mediaeval times in Britain, when the famous tansy puddings or cakes traditionally eaten after Lent were at their most popular. They were a kind of pancake and were thought to act as an internal springclean and tonic after winter ailments and lack of sun and warmth.

As a British and European native, tansy's bright yellow, long-lasting flowerheads used to be a common part of hedgerow and fieldside, but the herb is now rarely seen. The long-lasting qualities of its flowers may be commemorated in the name, which comes from the Greek *athanaton*, immortal. The flowers are said to be an excellent ingredient for embalming corpses. The pungent aroma of its flowerheads and leaves made it one of the most useful of insect repellents.

Cultivation Not a difficult plant to grow, but tansy needs, like sweet cicely, to be positioned with care, as the roots serve as a method of increase, and spread widely beneath the soil. Division of established plants is another common method of increase in spring or autumn; seed at the same season is a third method. Most soils and sites will suit it, except waterlogged soil; spacing should be about 45cm (18in). One or two plants do not look out of place in a border.

IDENTIFICATION

Height 60-90cm (2-3ft), spread 45cm (18in)
Root tough, fibrous, spreading, rhizomatous
Stem dark green, erect, grooved
Leaf dark green, pinnate, to 15cm (6in) long, deeply divided into toothed segments each 2.5-3cm (1-1½in) long, the whole leaf being about 10cm (4in) wide
Flower bright yellow button flowers 6mm (¼in) diameter, in flat umbel clusters, late summer-mid autumn
Seed light brown, tiny, without a pappus

USES

Culinary fresh or dried leaves, stems, flowers; use small quantities chopped for flavouring meat dishes, in salads, egg dishes including omelettes and pancakes, in cakes
Medicinal flowering stems, fresh or dried, in small quantities to help digestion, and to help in the treatment of roundworms; large quantities harmful, none should be taken in pregnancy
Cosmetic not so used
Domestic considerable insect-repellent properties, for strewing, in household linen, clothing, a fly deterrent, and said to repel garden insect pests; provides orange dye with chrome and cream of tartar
Fragrance and Aroma all parts strongly and bitterly aromatic

RECIPE

Tansy pancakes
The tansy pudding of mediaeval times is recorded in a recipe from *The Receipt Book of John Nott*, cook to the Duke of Bolton, 1723.
Take 7 eggs leaving out 2 whites, and a pint of cream, some Tansy, Thyme, Sweet Marjoram, Parsley, Strawberry leaves, all shred very small, a little nutmeg, add a plate of grated white bread, let these be mixed all together, then fry them but not too brown.
Here is a modern version of this recipe:
100g/4oz/1 cup plain flour
1 egg
pinch of salt
150ml/¼ pint/⅔ cup milk
1 dessertspoon chopped tansy leaves
butter for frying
sugar
Sift the flour into a bowl with the salt. Beat in the egg, the milk and then the chopped tansy leaves. Leave the mixture to stand for a little before using. Melt a little butter in a frying pan and use the batter to make 4 pancakes. Roll up and sprinkle with sugar.

tansy leaves

dried tansy leaves

tansy pancakes

Tarragon

There are two sorts of tarragon, French and Russian. The latter has a stronger, less pleasant flavour and coarser growth, with larger leaves; the French form is much to be preferred for its subtle flavour, but is so often replaced by the Russian, though labelled as French. From southern Europe, it can succumb to cold winters, and in any case should be renewed every three years as the flavour deteriorates with maturity of the plant.

Dracunculus is the Latin for a little dragon, and the common name is derived from *esdragon*, a French corruption of the Latin; this association with fabulous beasts is because it was thought to have considerable powers for healing the bites of snakes, serpents, and other venomous creatures. Alternatively, it may be because the roots were thought to coil and curve in the same way that a dragon's or snake's body does.

Cultivation Tarragon, more than most Mediterranean herbs, needs sun and good soil drainage, with shelter from cold wind. Given these conditions, it will flourish and may even, in the warmest gardens, flower and set seed; it will of course do so in warm temperate climates without difficulty. The roots, or rhizomes, spread widely, and each plant needs an area of 120cm (4ft) square, though the top growth will only cover about 60cm (2ft). These same rhizomes can be used for increase in spring, using short lengths with buds attached. Tip cuttings of young shoots will root in summer with warmth.

RECIPE

Sauce béarnaise
Tarragon is the essential ingredient in this famous French sauce which is usually served with distinctively flavoured fish, such as sole, salmon and shellfish. It also often accompanies roast lamb cooked in the French manner – slightly rare.
3-4 egg yolks
100-125g/4-5oz/½-¾ cup chilled butter, cut into small cubes
1 tbls chopped shallot or spring onion
2 tbls tarragon vinegar
4 tbls white wine
1 tbls chopped tarragon
salt and black pepper to taste
Put the white wine, vinegar, shallots, half the tarragon and black pepper into a small saucepan and boil down until 2 tablespoons of liquid is left. Allow the liquid to cool a little before putting it into the top of a double boiler (or a bowl or saucepan which will fit into an ordinary saucepan). The underneath saucepan should be half-filled with warm water and put on a gentle heat. The water should at no time be more than barely simmering – if it boils the sauce will get too hot and curdle. To the liquid in the top pan add the cubes of butter, a few at once, stirring all the time. When the butter is absorbed, add the beaten egg yolks and stir very carefully until the sauce thickens. Remove from the heat, add salt to taste and stir in the remainder of the chopped tarragon. The sauce is not intended to be served hot, but tepid.

COMPOSITAE *Artemisia dracunculus*
Herbaceous perennial

IDENTIFICATION

Height 60-90cm (2-3ft), spread 30-45cm (12-18in)
Root tapering, creeping, some fibrous roots also
Leaf dark green above, lighter beneath, narrow, slightly pointed, entire or minutely toothed, divided into three at the tip if basal, 2.5-7cm (1-3in) long, 3-6mm (⅛-¼in) wide, alternate
Flower inconspicuous, greenish, in loose clusters, July, but never open completely in cold temperate climates
Seed does not form in cool conditions, but is minute and without a pappus when it does

USES

Culinary fresh or dried leaf, sparingly in any meat dish, in salads, egg and cheese dishes, with tomatoes, mushrooms, sauces, herb butter, vinegar, with fish, sauce tartare
Medicinal none, though the root was once used for toothache
Cosmetic none
Domestic none
Fragrance and Aroma leaves strongly and sweetly aromatic, quite unlike any other herb; the oil is occasionally used in perfumery

dried tarragon leaves

tarragon leaves

béarnaise sauce

Thyme

IDENTIFICATION

Height up to 20cm (8in) tall, rarely 30cm (12in), and similar spread
Root many, fibrous on woody, central, anchoring root
Stem brown and woody at base, becoming thin and wiry, older stems twisted and gnarled
Leaf grey-green, very small, entire, long-oval to linear, 3-5mm (⅛-¼in) long, half as wide, opposite
Flower pale purple to lilac, tiny, two-lipped tubular, in clusters at the ends of shoots to cover the plant, June-July
Seed rounded, minute, brown

A stuffing for pork or chicken is not complete without thyme in it, and it is one of the most universal and most used herbs, its sharp, aromatic flavour adding distinction and quality to almost all savoury dishes. But there are many varieties of thyme, and two of particular culinary use are *T. × citriodorus*, lemon thyme, and *T. herba-barona* caraway thyme. *T. capitatus* has a markedly 'smoky' aroma, and is particularly attractive to bees, though all the thymes, when in flower, will be constantly visited. Lemon thyme comes into flower some weeks after garden thyme and, like it, is long in flower, so a constant procession of bees for at least two months can be assured where both species grow in the garden.

Thyme has considerable medicinal qualities, the main one being its antiseptic property, partly due to thymol. Historically, its use dates back to the classical ages, and it seems likely that the powerful *T. capitatus* which grows all over Greece, was the one used by the ancient Greeks. Introduced to general use in Britain by the Romans, thyme is mentioned in an old Anglo-Saxon text of the 10th century, and Gerard described *T. serpyllum*, creeping thyme, as did Culpeper, who recommended it for hang-overs: 'An infusion of the leaves removes the headache, occasioned by inebriation'.

Cultivation The thymes need to be hard-grown, to give their best flavour and aroma, so a poor stony soil on a slope, facing the sun, is the ideal site. Shelter from cold and cold winds is important, and in hard winters, thyme is unlikely to survive. It is easily increased from tip cuttings in summer, or by layering stems down round the plant, when they will readily root. It can stand a good deal of drought in summer.

USES

Culinary fresh or dried leaves, added to roast or grilled meat before cooking, kebabs, poultry, use in *fines herbes*, bouquet garni, cheese dishes, salads, marinades, vinegar and oil; lemon thyme in custards
Medicinal fresh or dried leaves, dried flowering plant, oil; strongly antiseptic, especially good for respiratory and intestinal ailments, as gargle and mouthwash, or wash for cuts, broken chilblains, grazes, etc., oil is a vermifuge, for digestion and an appetite stimulant
Cosmetic a deodorant, and for healing spots, pimples and similar skin problems, in washing water, toothpaste
Domestic burning to cleanse and perfume the air, in candles, in snuff, in household linen
Fragrance and Aroma strongly and warmly aromatic, oils used in soap and perfumery, leaves in potpourri, herb pillows

RECIPE

Thyme vinegar (for marinades, salads and sauces)
2 tbls fresh thyme leaves
1 sprig thyme
600ml/1 pint/2½ cups white wine vinegar
Crush the thyme leaves in a mortar. Heat the vinegar to almost boiling point (do not allow to boil) and pour over the leaves. Pour into a wide-necked bottle, seal tightly and stand in a dark place for 2-3 weeks. Strain into a clean bottle, add a sprig of thyme and stopper the bottle with a cork. Herb vinegars make ideal gifts.

chopped lemon thyme

thyme seeds

common thyme leaves and flowers

dried thyme

thyme vinegar

Valerian

IDENTIFICATION

Height 20-150cm (8-60in), spread 60cm (2ft)
Root stout, short, upright rhizome, with fibrous roots spreading sideways in the soil from it
Stem green, erect, round, hollow, slightly grooved, slightly hairy near base, unbranched
Leaf green, pinnate, 6-10 pairs of lance-shaped segments, toothed, each 5-7cm (2-3in) long, hairy beneath, lower leaves stalked, leaves in pairs
Flower white tinted pink, small, with five petal-like lobes to a tubular corolla, in clusters at the end of the stem, June-September
Seed tiny, oblong, brown, with a pappus

A herb whose main attribute is medicinal, valerian has a slightly unpleasant smell, especially when injured, but its relation *V.phu* (pronounced exactly as it appears) is very much more foetid.

The plant is indigenous to Europe including Britain, and northern Asia, and is now naturalized in North America. In the Middle Ages in Britain it was called 'all heal'; it was a common medicinal remedy at the time of Hippocrates in the 4th and 5th centuries B.C.; it was valued by the Romans, and both Gerard and Culpeper described it. Valerian was formerly used in the treatment of epilepsy, and has considerable properties for soothing, calming and acting as a sedative. The roots have an extraordinary fascination for cats, rats and earthworms.

Cultivation Valerian prefers damp soils, and is found growing wild in marshes and ditches, close to streams, and on the edges of ponds or lakes where moisture and nutrient are plentiful. Sun or some shade are equally acceptable. Increase is easiest by detaching runners with rooted plantlets attached, and such plants contain the greatest alkaloid content. Plants from seeds have less. If seed is used, it should be sown outdoors in April, uncovered, as it does not germinate in the dark, and all plants will need a final spacing of 60cm (2ft).

USES

Culinary none now, though once a flavouring
Medicinal dried rootstock, as a sedative and tranquillizer, for a variety of nervous troubles and for insomnia; should not be taken in large quantities over a long period of time
Cosmetic none
Domestic once used amongst clothing and household linen
Fragrance and Aroma whole plant, particularly root, has a nauseating smell

PRESCRIPTION

Valerian tea (for insomnia, as a mild sedative)
This tea can be made in the usual way, but it is more effective if taken when cold. Use 1 teaspoon valerian roots chopped small or grated to 1 cupful of boiling water. Leave the tea to stand for at least 2 hours. Then strain and use.

dried valerian root

valerian root & leaves

valerian tea

Vervain

Vervain was called 'holy herb' by the Romans, and it was used in religious rites by the Druids. It has strong associations with magic and superstition and was once considered a kind of cure-all. From the southern Mediterranean originally, it is now established in many other parts including Britain and North America where it grows in rough grass and in hedgerows and at roadsides.

Its main use is medicinal, and it is a powerful remedy in its field, but there is room for a good deal of research still on its constituents. Once reputed to have aphrodisiacal qualities, it was said by Gerard that many stories were heard 'of Vervaine tending to witchcraft and sorcery', and Culpeper reported so long a list of its healing virtues that it suggested no other medicine need be used.

Cultivation Seed sown in spring can be used to start a stock of vervain, and will do best in fertile but well-drained soil and sun, though it will grow on most sites. It can be divided for increase in late spring or autumn, or increased by tip cuttings in summer.

USES

Culinary not so used
Medicinal dried flowering plant, fresh or dried leaves, as a sedative tea; for digestion, nervous exhaustion, depression, for skin complaints, and to treat wounds
Cosmetic once thought to be a good eye-lotion
Domestic not so used
Fragrance and Aroma none

PRESCRIPTION

Vervain eye compress (for cleansing and soothing tired or inflamed eyes)
Make an infusion using 1 tablespoon of chopped vervain leaves to 150 ml/ ¼ pint/⅔ cup boiling water. Allow to cool and strain into a screwtop bottle. Soak cottonwool pads with the infusion and place over each eyelid. Leave for about 10 minutes before repeating the process, as necessary. Finally clean the eyes with fresh, cold water and pat dry.

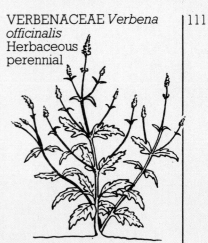

IDENTIFICATION

Height 30-90cm (1-3ft), spread 15-45cm (6-18in)
Root fibrous, spreading, some anchoring roots
Stem green, square, erect, wiry, somewhat branching, slightly hairy
Leaf green, toothed, lobed, shortly stalked, to 6cm (2¼in) long, opposite
Flower lilac, small, two-lipped tubular, sparse, at the end of shoots, in long spikes
Seed tiny, brown

vervain root & leaves

vervain seeds

vervain eye compress

dried vervain leaves

CRUCIFERAE *Cheiranthus cheiri*
Biennial, short-lived perennial

Wallflower

IDENTIFICATION

Height 30-60cm (1-2ft), spread 20-30cm (10-12in)
Root white tap root, fibrous spreading roots
Stem green, erect, hard and tough at base, smooth, much branched
Leaf green, entire, oblong lanceolate, 2.5-6.5cm (1-2½in) long
Flower various colours in the range orange, yellow, brown, scarlet, wine-red, in long clusters, 4-petalled, 1.2-2.5cm (½-1in) wide, mid-late spring
Seed small, round, black, in long narrow seed-case 7cm (3in) long

Although not regarded as a herb now, wallflowers were once thought to have medicinal uses and do in fact contain a strong constituent of the digitalis group. Their perfume is unique, and is particularly powerful in warm sunshine. They are not a native British plant, being indigenous to central Europe, but have spread throughout Europe and can be found from year to year as short-lived perennials in sheltered stony places in Britain where the winters are mild.

It once had the pretty name of *cherisaunce*, meaning 'comfort' as it was carried for its fragrance at fetes and parties during the Middle Ages, and it was in the 14th century in Scotland that it acquired the legend of faithfulness, from its use in an elopement. Far from being a disgrace at a dance, a 'wallflower' was a symbol of loyalty and constant love, and anyone who carried or wore one was regarded with respect.

Cultivation Seed is sown in late spring or early summer, in a nursery bed, and then either thinned twice to a final 10cm (4in) spacing, or thinned once to 2.5cm (1in) and then transplanted to another site in July. In either case the small plants are put into their flowering position early in mid autumn, 23cm (9in) apart. The tip of the main shoot and subsequent sideshoots should be nipped out to make the plant bushy and hence more floriferous. Wallflowers must have good soil drainage, otherwise they will die over winter with prolonged wet at their roots, and they also need a sunny place. In choosing their site, be guided by their common name.

USES

Culinary not so used
Medicinal none, though a flower conserve once used for apoplexy, and the oil for ague
Cosmetic not so used
Domestic not so used
Fragrance and Aroma strong sweet fragrance from flowers, used in potpourri, oil used in perfumery

RECIPE

Spring Potpourri (Dry)
5 parts tulip petals
5 parts scented spring flowers, e.g. wallflowers, lilac hyacinth, yellow azalea (Rhododendron lutea), violets and Brompton stocks
1 part rosemary flowers and leaves
⅙ part powdered allspice
half that quantity powdered cloves
little grated nutmeg
⅙ part powdered orris root and gum benzoin, mixed up to 10 drops wallflower oil
All the flowers and leaves should be dried; the tulips are for colour. Mix all well with a wooden spoon and add the oil, drop at a time until the fragrance is to your satisfaction. Allow three weeks from blending before use, stirring occasionally during this time.

wallflower seeds

wallflower leaves

wallflower

spring potpourri

Yarrow

Owners of lawns will know of yarrow as a tough and pernicious weed which resists all attempts to liquidate it. It adopts a flat and creeping habit of growth, thus enabling it to escape the mower.

But the ancients held it in great esteem because of its excellent properties for stopping bleeding; its generic name is said to come from the Greek hero Achilles, who used it on his soldier's wounds during the Trojan War. It was once called *herba militaris*, the military herb. The common name is a corruption of the Anglo-Saxon name *gearwe*.

Yarrow is native to Europe including Britain and is a commonly found wayside plant of field and trackway, with attractively feathery leaves and white flowers. Hybrids have been bred for the garden with grey-green or silvery foliage and deep or light yellow flowers as 'Moonshine' or 'Gold Plate', and a crimson one called 'Cerise Queen'. *A. clavenae* has white flowers on 15cm (6in) stems, and silver leaves. All are remarkably long-lasting in flower.

Cultivation Easily grown in any soil and situation, yarrow can be increased by division of the creeping root system in spring or autumn. The garden forms are more self-contained and less likely to get out of hand; they can be increased in the same way.

USES

Culinary use fresh leaves in salads
Medicinal fresh leaves, applied to wounds, said to have astringent and healing properties; dried leaves, stems, flowers, of use in dysentery, diarrhoea, for reducing high temperature; combine with peppermint and elderflowers to relieve colds. N.B. large doses induce headaches and giddiness
Cosmetic said to prevent baldness, if the head is washed with a decoction; an astringent for greasy skin
Domestic helps garden compost heaps to rot down as a natural activator; concentrated solution will provide a good fertilizer
Fragrance and Aroma leaves strongly aromatic

PRESCRIPTION

Yarrow infusion (for minor cuts and wounds)

(Recipe on page 138/9)

COMPOSITAE *Achillea millefolium*
Hardy perennial

IDENTIFICATION

Height 10-60cm (4-24in), spread 10cm (4in)
Root tough, stoloniferous, far-spreading, forming mats
Stem upright, pale green, angular, rough
Leaf dark green, downy feathery, up to 10cm (4in) long and 2.5cm (1in) wide, alternate
Flower white, pinkish or lilac, tiny, somewhat daisy-like but with only 5 rays, in loose, flat-headed clusters at the end of the stems, early-summer to late autumn
Seed tiny, inconspicuous

dried yarrow leaves

yarrow leaves & flowers

yarrow infusion

yarrow compress

Harvesting, drying and storage

In Provence, France, herbs are harvested and dried commercially, mostly for export. When buying dried herbs, it is worth seeking out Provençal herbs since they are more aromatic than those grown in northern regions.

The oils which give herbs their delightful aromas and flavours are volatile, i.e. they will readily escape from leaves, stems, seeds or other parts once these have been injured, and will then be further reduced by evaporation. Moreover, any cuts, bruises or other injuries to plants result in oxidation of the injured surface by the oxygen in the air, thus also changing the aroma and flavour.

Harvesting herbs

So, one of the important points to note in harvesting herbs for storage is to avoid injuring them as far as possible. Gather the part required gently; cut whole stems rather than single leaves or flowers; lay them in single layers on trays, racks, or in shallow wooden vegetable boxes, and take them into the storage area quickly, otherwise cover with dark cloth or paper. Try not to pile them up to any degree, as it does not take many minutes before even a small heap warms up, and starts the process of fermentation and decomposition. Try to keep each species separate in the tray, so that they do not contaminate each other, and pick only the quantity that can be dried in the drying area comfortably, without crowding.

Pick herbs which are clean, free from pest or disease, and not discoloured or damaged in any way already. If they are dirty, sponge them quickly and lightly with cool water and pat dry with kitchen paper.

When to harvest herbs

A second point to remember for maximum flavour and oil content is the time at which to harvest herbs: the time of day, the season, and the stage of growth. During the day, the morning is best, when the dew has evaporated so that the plants are dry, but before the sun is at its most intense, i.e. the early morning when the temperature is merely warm.

Choice of season depends to some extent on the part and species to be harvested, but is mostly from early summer onwards. Leaves have their greatest oil content just before the flowers open; flowers are at their best when barely opened. Seeds are collected just as they ripen, and roots dug in early-mid autumn as growth ceases and when they contain the food manufactured through a complete growing season.

So summer and autumn generally see the harvesting of some part of one herb or other every week, but there are exceptions, and these are noted in the Harvesting and Preserving chart (pages 134–137).

The leaves are the part required for the majority of culinary herbs, but the seeds often have highly individual flavours. The flowers contribute dyes in some cases as well as perfume; roots can be eaten as a vegetable, or contain the essential medicinal constituent, and there are instances where the stems are the important part. Sometimes it is necessary to use the entire flowering plant, but whichever part is employed, is also shown in the chart mentioned above.

Herbs which are to work for their living, and are not grown purely for garden decoration, will be wanted for use all year round, not a difficulty in warm temperate and tropical climates. But there are quite a number in cool temperate areas which either die down in autumn, for instance herbaceous perennials, or are annuals or biennials which die completely at the end of summer. Those which are grown for their foliage and which retain it all year are not a problem, and there are some which come into leaf as early as late winter and continue until late autumn, and yet others whose top growth can be kept growing for most if not all the year with the help of a gently-heated conservatory or greenhouse.

But flowers and seeds are only available at certain seasons whatever the climate, and roots can only be obtained at the expense of the top growth. Some form of preservation is necessary for many herbs, whether it is drying or freezing, and the techniques involved from harvest to final storage should be carefully followed for full conservation of the essential oils.

Drying herbs

In order to dry the plants with minimum loss of volatile oils they need warmth, darkness and air. Temperature should ideally be between 21° and 33°C (70° and 90°F), never above 36°C (95°F), that is, always slightly below body temperature. Herbs dry at different rates and one has to keep an eye on them to prevent them drying too quickly. The time will vary from two to three days to a week, depending on the part and the species.

An airy place is important, so that the moisture evaporating from the herbs can be dispersed quickly, and darkness is essential, to prevent oxidation of the material with consequent change in flavour and oil content. The domestic airing cupboard, an attic immediately under the roof in summer, provided it does not get too hot, an oven with a low temperature setting and the door ajar, a plate warming compartment, an electric dryer for washing, or an outhouse with a warm-air fan, are suitable drying areas, provided the temperature can be maintained between the limits noted.

Material should be spread out in single layers on trays, or on slatted wooden racks covered with muslin or netting, and the trays or frames placed in the drying area so that they have air circulating beneath as well as on top. The shallow wooden boxes with raised corners used for tomatoes and other vegetables or fruits such as peaches or grapes, are ideal as they can be stacked on top of each other and still allow for ventilation.

Alternatively the stems, roots or flowers can be tied in small bundles and hung, upside down in the case of stems and flowers, from a clothes-line, provided there is still good air circulation.

The length of drying time varies from herb to herb, and in general a good guide to completion of the process is in the state of the plant material. Leaves will be brittle and crisp, and will break easily into small pieces, but should not be reduced to a powdery state when touched. Stems should break sharply – if they still have a tendency to bend, they need further drying. Roots must be brittle and dry right through: any softness or sponginess means incomplete drying.

Seeds are slightly tricky to harvest as the final ripening occurs very quickly and they fall off and are scattered round the parents. If a few seeds fall when the plants are tapped, then they are ready for collection. Change in colour is also an indication of approaching maturity, and some also change their aroma. Seeds should be dried without any artificial heat in an airy place. The almost ripe seed-heads can be hung up in paper bags so that the majority of the seeds will fall into the bag as they mature. Seeds need to be thoroughly dried before storage and this can take up to two weeks.

Quick drying methods

Some herbs can be dried in the oven in a matter of 3-6 hours. The oven temperature should be no more than 36°C (95°F) and for sensitive herbs such as basil and chervil it should never exceed 30°C (90°F). Herbs should be placed on perforated sheets of brown paper and the oven door should be left ajar to allow moisture to escape. Check the drying herbs regularly to see that they are not overheating.

Microwave ovens have also been used for herb drying.

Left: Elderberries are usually harvested in the late summer after the plant's flowerheads, which can be dried, have been picked in midsummer. Fresh elderberries can be successfully stored in a deep freeze or used immediately to make jams, jellies, syrups and wine.

Above and right: Harvesting lavender in the south of France. Lavender is well adapted to the stony soil of Provence and Vaucluse and is grown extensively as a crop for the French perfume industry.

Herbs with small leaves such as rosemary and thyme take about one minute, while larger, moist leaves like mint and basil dry in about three minutes.

Storing dried herbs

It is often advised that dried leaves be broken into tiny pieces before storage, but even this can deplete the content of volatile oils, and it is better to store dried material as whole leaves, or in as large pieces as possible until the time of use. Before storing, remove all the unwanted material, chaff from seeds, loose pieces of stem; use a fine-mesh sieve if necessary. If leaves have to be reduced to tea leaf size at once, for making herbal teas such as chamomile or peppermint, a coffee-bean grinder or the grinder attachment to an electric mixer, or just crushing them with a rolling pin, will do the job.

Dried material must be stored in the dark, so containers which exclude light completely are ideal; dark-brown bottles or jars are suitable, and it is worth keeping medicine bottles, and other dark-coloured jars which are right for size and colouring. They must also be airtight, and containers should be filled completely initially, and plain paper used to fill the space that appears in the container as the herbs are used. The herbs should not be kept longer than six months or so, as even with all these precautions, they will lose most of their potency, and will begin to smell hay-like after this time.

Store each herb in a separate container, unless they are to make up, for instance, mixed herbs, bouquet garni, or your own favourite mixtures for marinades, or fines herbes. Label the containers at once and put the date on them.

If light-excluding containers cannot be found, paint the containers you do have black, or cover them with black paper, or keep the boxes or bottles in the dark, in a drawer or cupboard.

Freezing herbs

The modern alternative to drying, if there is a deep freeze available, is to freeze the herbs in a variety of ways. This has the advantage that they can be done as soon as picked, and the rapidity of the freezing also ensures better retention of the flavour or aroma, but it does only apply to leaves, flowers and soft stems.

Sprigs of the herbs to be frozen can be put in small loose bundles in polythene bags immediately they are cut and before they wilt. They should be labelled, the bag sealed and put straight into the freezer – there is no need to blanch them first. If they are to be used as mixtures, as suggested earlier, they can be frozen already made up for convenience, and all can go into the casserole, marinade or other dish without thawing. Alternatively, they can be chopped up while still frozen, and then used, although such herbs are not suitable for garnishing, as they will have lost their crisp, fresh appearance.

But herbs can be chopped up fresh and then frozen, if preferred, in water contained in the ice-cube-making tray. Cubes can then be used separately as required, and these can also be put straight into the dish concerned. Single whole leaves or flowers can be frozen in each cube, and the cubes added to winter wine punches and cordials for decoration and flavouring.

Fragrance and aroma

Fragrance is associated with beauty, smell with ugliness, yet both are odours. Is it nature's way of warning us of possible danger? Smells, unpleasant odours, come from rotting vegetation or animal matter, both of which are likely to be toxic, whereas fragrance is mostly given off by beautiful parts of plants. Of course, there are exceptions to these generalizations – there are some flowers which smell exactly like decaying meat, and unmentionable animal parts which supply prized perfumes.

Historical uses of fragrance

But it does seem that fragrance is associated with pleasure and for health, and it is a pity that sweet-smelling perfumes are not now in everyday use in the home, as they were in the past. The Romans, great sybarites that they were, had perfumed doves flying above banquets; they scattered tons of rose petals on festival days, and sprayed their rooms with perfumed oils, in spite of the fact that Caesar regarded perfume as effeminate and made its sale illegal.

The Greeks thought perfume was divine in origin, and the ancient Egyptians, who originally confined the use of perfume to religious rituals, gradually allowed its personal use until it became an essential part of the toilet. From Rome its use spread throughout northern and western Europe to Britain, and thence eventually to the New World in the sixteenth and seventeenth centuries by the first settlers. There, it must have met the long-standing tradition of herbal medicine practised by the Indian tribes already established, who would have appreciated the therapeutic use of aromatic oils.

In mediaeval times in Britain, and even more so in Europe, aromatic and fragrant herbs had a hundred everyday uses. One has a vague impression that those times and later, perhaps up to the end of the eighteenth century, were distinguished by a general lack of hygiene; dirt, smells, fleas, sores, boils and skin complaints in general were commonplace things. Yet, in fact people had a good deal of natural material available to overcome all these. For most people life was a rural one, and many families probably had a little bit of ground outside their homes on which to grow plants. For those that had not, there were many herbs which were native plants growing wild and in much greater quantity than they do now.

It would have been a common habit to strew aromatic and fragrant leaves on floors to combat insects, to use them in all one's clothes and household linen, and to burn sprigs of such plants in various rooms to offset unpleasant odours, or simply to provide a sweet fragrance. Finger bowls contained flower petals, gloves were perfumed, pomanders and tussie mussies were carried, and scented candles burnt. Lavender was used in washing water, and potpourris were an essential part of everyday life. Furniture polish was perfumed.

Perfume as such consisted at first of the simple natural oils, such as rosemary, sage and lavender, but those with an alcoholic base began to make their appearance in the fourteenth century, with the production of Hungary Water. It is of note that a writer of 1560, described an English home thus: 'the neat cleanliness, the pleasant and delightful furniture, wonderfully rejoiced me; their chambers and parlours strewed over with sweet herbs, refreshed me'. Gerard described meadowsweet as far excelling 'All other strewing herbs, to decke up houses, to straw in chambers, halls and banqueting houses in the Summer time; for the smell thereof makes the heart merrie, delighteth the senses'.

It would do no harm, and probably a great deal of good, to follow some of these practices, in scenting our homes, or parts of them; it might even be possible to use them in the same way that colour is, to create a certain mood – for instance, for soothing and tranquillizing in resting rooms, for stimulating in living-rooms, and for 'making the heart merry' at dinner-parties.

How we detect fragrance

Odours of any kind are detected by a small piece of lining

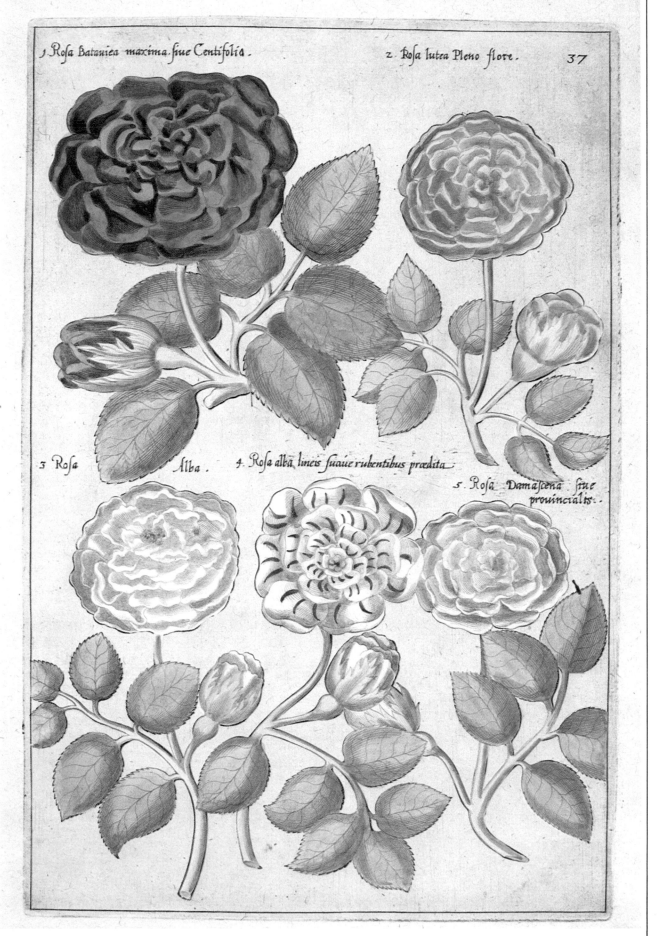

1. Rosa Batauica maxima. siue Centifolia.　　2. Rosa lutea Pleno flore.　37

3. Rosa　　　Alba.　　4. Rosa albā lineis suaue rubentibus prædita.

5. Rosa Damascena siue prouincialis.

membrane at the top of the nose cavity. On the surface of this there are olfactory 'hairs' which connect with a nerve fibre ultimately in contact with the central nervous system. If these filaments are covered with a thicker layer of mucous fluid than normal, as with catarrh, or if this layer is replaced with a dry one, the ability to distinguish between smells is reduced or even temporarily destroyed.

Different reactions to smells and perfumes, when some people cannot detect any odour, and others different odours, is probably due to one's genes, though smoking can interfere, and prolonged sniffing blunts the ability. Incidentally, the Latin for 'to smoke' is *fumere*; *par* or *per* means 'through'; perhaps perfume is so-called because herbs were burnt for various reasons. *Fragrans* originally meant simply 'smelling' and its meaning of sweetness is a modern one.

There are said to be only seven primary odours: ethereal, camphoraceous, musky, floral, pepperminty, pungent and putrid, and all other odours are compounds of these; almond, for example, is a mixture of floral, camphoraceous and peppperminty ingredients.

Methods of extracting perfume
The art of perfumery is extremely complex, and the professional perfumer has literally thousands of sources of fragrance on which to call when blending a new perfume. In general, perfumes are based on a solvent such as oil or pure alcohol and it is possible, in spite of the potential for complexity, to make one's own perfumes based on the flowers and/or leaves of herbs in the same way that potpourris can be satisfactorily made. Pure alcohol is usually not obtainable, but a good substitute is isopropyl alcohol, and for oil, any vegetable oil can be used, though olive or sweet almond will give a better product. They will keep longer if 10 per cent of wheatgerm oil can be added, after infusing.

There are four main methods of extracting the perfume or, more precisely the essential oil which contains the perfume or aroma of a plant: *distillation, extraction* (with alcohol or volatile solvents), *maceration* and *enfleurage*. A fifth is *expression*, used largely on fruit, in which considerable pressure is exerted to squeeze out the oil. For perfumes made at home, maceration and enfleurage are the most practicable methods to try out.

Maceration in effect is the way in which attar of roses is said to have been discovered. The story is that a Persian princess and her bridegroom were rowing on a lake after the wedding in which rose petals had been prodigally used, and the surface of the lake became covered with them. The princess, trailing her hands in the water, discovered that they were covered in a sweet-smelling oil, and so the method and the perfume were born. At home, it is simply a case of steeping fresh flower petals or other scented material in water, topping up with new material until sufficient oil is obtained, and then extracting it with isopropyl alcohol.

Enfleurage involves the use of fat applied to perfectly clean sheets of glass. Each sheet is held in a wooden frame, of any convenient size, and fat or grease spread over each surface. The flowers or other scented material are pressed into the fat, without the stems, and left in a dark place for 24 hours, when fresh flowers are used to replace the old. This continues until the flowers are no longer available. In this way the fat absorbs the perfumed oil and then becomes a pomade; the oil can be extracted with alcohol.

Alternatively, olive oil can be used, placing it in a bottle and filling the bottle with the scented material. After 24 hours in a warm dark place, the flowers and oil should be strained through a net or muslin (cheesecloth) bag and the resultant oil, now slightly perfumed, placed in a second bottle, and again filled with flowers. This can be repeated until there are no more flowers available. Then an equal quantity of isopropyl alcohol is added and the mixture shaken together thoroughly every day for three to four weeks. The alcohol will then extract the essential oil and be perfumed. However, the now-perfumed olive oil can be left as it is, and used as an after-bath oil. Roses, lavender, honeysuckle, clove pinks and wallflowers can all be tried for perfume.

For aromatic oils for cooking, rosemary, tarragon, marjoram, sage and thyme can also be soaked in the oil, using complete sprigs. Use freshly dried material in this case, to avoid cloudy oil, and again keep it warm-hot; the higher the temperature, the quicker will the extraction occur.

Potpourris and how to make them
The art of potpourri-making became sadly lost until recently, but with the renewal of interest in herbs and all things herbal, many of the old recipes are being revived together with detailed directions for preparing the contents, and putting them together.

The word 'potpourri' literally means 'rotten pot', and is derived from the French *pot* and *pourrir*, to rot. Originally such a mixture contained what were regarded as disinfectant herbs: rosemary, lavender, sage, southernwood, and they were mixed with spices, oils and fixatives, and left in a closed container to mature or 'rot' into a moist mixture, strongly aromatic and long-lasting. Later, perfumed material became popular, and gradually replaced the original formulae.

Potpourris now basically consist of the material to be used, whether it is flowers or leaves to which spices and fixatives are added, and sometimes also essential oils. The spices may be such seeds, fruits, roots, etc., as coriander, caraway, cinnamon, cloves, nutmeg or ginger; fixatives include orris root, sweet flag root (calamus), sandalwood, common salt, or bay salt (that is, sea salt), and the essential oils can be any extracted from perfumed flowers, from the aromatic herbs and citrus fruits, and from the fragrant timbers.

Dry potpourris
The dry version of potpourri is the one most often made at home or available in stores, and is easier to make, as well as

being visually more attractive than the moist kind which, however, lasts longer and is stronger and more penetrating. Dry potpourri consists of petals and leaves dried in the same way that culinary herbs are, and collected at the same time of day and in the same condition. Darkness is especially important to preserve the colour of the flowers. The material should be crisp but not powdery when finally ready, and may take a day, or a week or longer to reach the right stage; it can be added to as the season goes on.

All are mixed together in, preferably, a glazed earthenware container or at any rate not a metal one, the spices then added and also thoroughly mixed in, and then the essential oil, drop by drop, depending on the fragrance achieved already. A dry potpourri relies in the last analysis on the added spices and oils for the strength and lasting qualities of its fragrance.

The spices should be ground up very finely, and for this a pepper mill, coffee grinder or heavy pestle and mortar are suitable. For the oil, use a syringe or eye-dropper.

Moist potpourris

Moist potpourri uses petals and leaves which are only part-dried, so that they are slightly flabby and limp, a little bit like moist chamois leather. The drying method is the same, but stops much sooner – you may need to examine the material more frequently to prevent it from drying too much.

It takes longer to complete, as several months are required for maturation. Quite a lot of salt will be needed, in the proportion of 3 parts petals and leaves to 1 of salt. Put a layer of petals an inch (2.5 cm) thick in the bottom of the container, and cover with the salt sprinkled evenly all over it and firmed down, and repeat these two layers until all the current supply of material is used up. Keep the layers pressed down hard and weighted well, and continue to add salt and flowers as they become available, stirring the material already in the container thoroughly before adding the new.

If liquid appears at the bottom of the container, drain it off and use it in the bath, and if frothing occurs, stir the mix to absorb it. When the container is full, there will be a caked mass of petals and leaves. Break this up with a fork and then add to it a mixture of spices, and a mixture, made up separately, of dried herbs and citrus peel, sprinkling all over the potpourri and blending them thoroughly and gradually. At this stage, the mix will be strongly aromatic, and a drop or two of essential oil of your choice may be necessary, but often no further additions are needed.

This final mix is then returned to the container, tightly pressed down and the container covered, mainly to keep out dust, but it should not be airtight. After about six weeks, the finally matured perfume will be apparent, and will then last for years. It is usually kept in a closed jar and opened when the fragrance is required to scent a room.

Soaps, scented potpourris, rose petals, herbal waters and oils are still used today, as they were in ancient times. Fragrant essences and oils, extracted commercially from lavender, roses, honeysuckle and many other herbs, have wide application in the perfume and cosmetic industries.

Tussie mussies and lavender sachets, as well as herbal oils and vinegars, are delightful gifts which can be easily made in the home.

Fragrant gifts

Recipes for potpourris, fragrant and aromatic oils, and culinary vinegars will be found in the descriptive list of herbs (pages 44–113), but in addition to these, the following make delightful gifts, and are easily made.

Orange pomander

Use a thin-skinned orange, and make a narrow slit in the skin round the circumference, removing about 6 mm (¼ in) width, then make another at right-angles to this, so that the orange is marked in quarters. Put the orange in a warm place for a day or two to dry out, then push whole cloves into it closely enough to ensure that the heads are virtually touching. Use a thin knitting-needle to make holes if the orange is tough. When the whole orange is covered, roll it in a mixture of powdered orris root alone, or a mixture with spices of your choice, such as cinnamon, ginger, mixed spice, etc., and then

wrap it up for two weeks and store in the dark. Take off the wrapping, tie coloured ribbon round the orange over the cut sections, and use for hanging in cupboard or wardrobe.

Scented sachets
For these, use lavender, or the dried version of potpourri, or make up your own mixtures of aromatic herbs, depending on whether you want them for fragrance or for warding off moths and other insects from clothes and household linen.

Lavender should be cut just before the flowers are fully open, and hung upside down for a few days to dry, then rubbed down to remove the flowers. Used alone it is a pungent fragrance, long-lasting and pervading. Insect-repellent mixtures can contain any of the following: costmary, southernwood, tansy, rue, rosemary, mint, all crushed, and powdered cloves, in whatever combination you prefer.

Make up the small bags to contain them from muslin (cheesecloth) or nylon net or any thin material in pretty designs; pack them fairly tight, and finish with ribbons or cords. They should remain effective for one to two years.

Tussie mussie
This is a tiny bunch or nosegay of fragrant flowers and herbs, principally used in mediaeval times for carrying in the hand and warding off unpleasant smells and infection from plague and other diseases. The formal Victorian posies were a derivation, but by then were merely a pretty conceit to provide decoration and perfume. As a modern gift they can be made up, using small, perfect blooms, fresh leaves, with perhaps a rose bud or pink as the centre, and the outside finished off with a white paper doily and secured with ribbon. It should be as neat and formal as possible, with the blooms arranged in concentric circles, interleaved with foliage. Diameter should be about 6-7 cm (2½-3 in).

Wild herbs

Herbs were originally all wild plants; in fact many of the plants now grown in gardens are wild plants in their native countries, and are not the result of many years of plant breeding and hybridizing under cultivation. The blue morning glory, for instance, with its exquisitely shaded, blue trumpet flowers is a rampant invader in its native South Africa, as the British white-funneled bindweed is an obstinate and recalcitrant colonizer of herbaceous borders, shrubs and roses.

Beneficial weeds

Another name for wild plants which appear unwantedly in gardens is 'weed' but many, if not all, of these so-called weeds once had considerable value medicinally, to say nothing of their household and domestic merits. Practically any plant seen during country rambles, by the pathside, in pastures and meadows, growing in hedges and at the side of streams and ponds, probably had some significance to the 'infirmarers' and physicians of the past.

Mugwort, *Artemisia vulgaris*, is one, once used to flavour all sorts of drinks, particularly home-made beer, to ward off moths, and as a cold preventative; it is a common weed of wasteland. Eyebright, *Euphrasia officinalis*, is another, a small unremarkable plant, easily trampled underfoot on paths, and with tiny white and lilac tubular flowers – it is a member of the *Scrophulariaceae*. It was thought by Arab physicians to cure 'all evils of the eye', and Gerard said that 'it preserves the sight, and being feeble and lost it restores the same'.

Cowslips (*Primula veris*) were used to remedy restlessness, insomnia and in general act as a sedative; the red or corn poppy of Flanders (*Papaver rhoeas*) is still a remedy for many ailments including tonsillitis, anxiety and coughs. Various species of thistles have been employed for all sorts of needs, for making paper, curdling milk, as a tonic, and diaphoretic, and so on. Weed herbs in the descriptive list of herbs (pages 44–113) include dandelion, nettle, elder, horsetail, marshmallow, mullein and valerian.

Couch-grass, that curse of the gardener and nightmare amongst shrubs and herbaceous perennials, was formerly much used for a variety of ailments including cystitis and rheumatism, has a diuretic effect, and is still a urinary antiseptic.

Ground-elder is another invader bent on taking over the whole garden, but its other name of 'goutweed' gives the game away; it, too, was once a valued herb supposed to have great affects on gout and sciatica, though even in Elizabethan times, was often regarded as a nuisance – Gerard says that 'when it hath once taken root, it will hardly be gotten out againe, to the annoyance of better herbs.' It could not be better described. Its very commonness is indicated by the number of vernacular names it has, at least sixteen, amongst which is 'bishop's-weed', because it was so often found near ruined churches, monasteries and similar buildings, having been introduced by the mediaeval monks as a herb of healing.

Even the ubiquitous bramble or blackberry had its place; apart from its delicious jelly and fruits – the jelly was once used to good effect in cases of dropsy – the bark and roots were considered of much value in treating diarrhoea and dysentery, and the leaves are still recommended as a decoction for treating external ulcers and as a gargle; they are thought to have an anti-diabetic effect, though this is not yet proven.

A country walk, then, can easily turn into a voyage of discovery if you take a modern herbal with you, or alternatively make notes in advance from a herbal, of wild plants which used to be herbs, and take a flora for identification. If you have no herbal, take a notebook to enable you to put down details of the plants found, together with sketches or photographs. These will enable you to check with a library copy whether the plants discovered have a history of ancient use, and perhaps a modern one. You will find the old dye plants, those used for shampoos and hair

colouring, for skin cleansing, healing, poultices – an endless number for human needs and remedies.

Poisonous herbs

But a word of warning: there are also some wild plants once used herbally as emetics, purgatives and laxatives, which are now known to be poisonous. Don't experiment too far with flavours of berries or leaves – if in doubt, don't try it. The following are poisonous wild plants commonly found growing in Britain and North America:
Atropa belladonna, deadly nightshade; *Bryonia dioica*, white bryony; *Colchicum autumnale*, autumn crocus; *Aconitum anglicum*, monk's hood; *Conium maculatum*, hemlock; *Datura stramonium*, thornapple; *Helleborus niger*, Christmas rose; *Mandragora officinalis*, mandrake; *Mercurialis perennis*, dog mercury; *Solanum dulcamara*, woody nightshade; *Solanum nigra*, black nightshade.

Gardeners' friends

It is also worth remembering that herbal 'weeds' may well do good to one's garden plants, provided they can be kept under reasonable control. A light weed cover will keep the soil moist for longer, and provide shade for roots. Hoeing such a cover in before it flowers and seeds provides a kind of instant green manure which improves or maintains a good soil structure. Chamomile is said to be the plants' doctor – in some way the secretions given off by the roots help unhealthy young plants to recover.

Red clover, *Trifolium pratense*, will add to the nitrogen content of the soil, and pieces of the hollow stems of angelica will trap earwigs. Compost material can be encouraged to rot down by adding nettle tops to it, and valerian, dandelion leaves, chamomile and yarrow leaves mixed together with nettles form a ready-made accelerator used in thin layers as the heap is built.

Create your own nature reserve

If there is enough space to spare in the garden from growing ornamentals and fruit/vegetable crops, it is a good idea to turn it into a kind of controlled nature reserve, in which weeds or wild herbs can be left to grow naturally, without any particular plan of planting. Naturally, the more rampant varieties such as bramble, bindweed, nettle, ground-elder and horsetail will need checking, but if these are likely to be a problem, don't introduce them. Stick to the smaller herbaceous and annual plants, such as scarlet pimpernel, corn poppy, chickweed (*Stellaria media*), wild marjoram, alexanders, burdock, wild chicory, foxglove, meadowsweet, soapwort, teasel, and dyer's weld (*Reseda luteola*), to name just a few.

You can have a pretty nature reserve without much difficulty – paths in it could consist of clover, yarrow and chamomile, clipped occasionally, or even mown – and the flowering plants could be mixed with various grasses for a completely natural effect. Such a mixture is what has come to be called a flowering meadow, which is left untouched except for cutting immediately after the majority of plants have flowered, usually about the middle of midsummer. This ensures seeding for next year and encourages the greatest number of species. The cut material should be left to lie.

But you can alternatively just grow the flowering wild plants, and be a little more formal, and at the same time more decorative, by planting them in beds, so that the contrast between this section and the rest of the garden is not so great. Some of the prettiest varieties are: yellow archangel,

Above: Hemlock, one of the most common poisonous plants, is often found growing in roadside ditches and on waste ground and bears a dangerous resemblance to cow parsley. Socrates is said to have been killed with the juice of this herb.

Right: Poppies, nettles and chamomile, all plants with useful properties, growing in attractive profusion by a roadside.

Below: Elder in flower in midsummer beside a farm building. Elder grows as rapidly as most weeds unless it is kept under control by pruning.

Overleaf: Although cowslip is a common plant in fields, meadows and hedgerows, it was once used medicinally for restlessness, insomnia and, in general, as a sedative.

Lamiastrum galeobdolon; bellflower, *Campanula trachelium*; bluebell, *Endymion non-scriptus*; broom, *Cytisus scoparius*; dyers greenwood, *Genista tinctoria*; bugle, *Ajuga reptans*; meadow buttercup, *Ranunculus acris*; red campion, *Silene dioica*; greater celandine, *Chelidonium majus*; lesser celandine, *Ranunculus ficaria*; wild chicory *Cichorium intybus* cowslip, *Primula veris*.

There are also dandelion, evening primrose, foxglove, harebell, heart's ease, herb robert, purple loosestrife, mullein, ox-eye daisy, field scabious, devil's bit, sea holly, tansy, teasel, thistles, thrift and yellow rattle, practically all of which have had or still have some herbal use.

Birds, bees and other fauna

You will also find that, by growing all these native plants, you will attract a good many other living species, representatives of the insect, animal, bird and aquatic orders, particularly butterflies, moths, pollinating insects generally such as bees, hoverflies and lacewings; species of birds, probably never seen in the garden before, as they discover seeds or berries which are part of their essential diet; frogs and toads, newts and, if you sink a pond, water snails, water beetles and other aquatics. A heap of mown hay and leaves will encourage hedgehogs to hibernate; voles, field mice and perhaps even dormice will appear.

The average suburban garden is something of a nature reserve in its own right, and insects alone that can be seen in it may consist of over 200 species of moths, more than 80 sorts of bees and wasps, and nearly two dozen butterflies. Hoverflies, also called flower flies, in particular may be abundant – getting on for 100 different species, and these not only do no harm, but do a great deal of good, partly by pollinating, and partly by the larvae feeding on greenfly. Moths mostly fly and feed after dark, in particular at dusk and dawn, and the garden or nature reserve which contains an abundance of scented plants, especially those whose perfume comes out at night, will attract moths in quantity, and of course their larvae, the caterpillars.

A patch of garden or meadow devoted to this kind of plant may cause visitors to wonder why you have allowed it to revert to a wilderness. However, the good that it will do to the rest of the garden in restoring and maintaining a natural balance, and the fact that native plants are being conserved and increased, more than justify its presence. Indeed, in the modern world, such areas are now essential if plant, animal and insect species are not to disappear for ever.

Botanical/common herb names

Botanic	English
Achillea millefolium	Yarrow
Allium sativum	Garlic
Allium schoenoprasum	Chives
Aloysia triphylla syn. *Lippia citriodora*	Lemon verbena
Althaea officinalis	Marshmallow
Anethum graveolens	Dill, dillweed
Angelica archangelica	Angelica
Anthemis nobilis see *Chamaemelum nobile*	
Anthriscus cerefolium	Chervil
Armoracia rusticana syn. *Cochlearia armoracia*	Horseradish
Artemisia abrotanum	Southernwood, lad's love, old man
Artemisia dracunculus	Tarragon, French tarragon
Borago officinalis	Borage, bee bread
Brassica nigra	Mustard (black)
Calendula officinalis	Marigold
Carum carvi	Caraway
Chamaemelum nobile syn. *Anthemis nobilis*	Common, Roman or double chamomile
Cheiranthus cheiri	Wallflower
Chrysanthemum balsamita	Costmary, alecost, bible leaf
Chrysanthemum parthenium	Feverfew, featherfew
Cochlearia armoracia see *Armoracia rusticana*	
Coriandrum sativum	Coriander
Dianthus caryophyllus	Pink, clove pink, clove July, gillyflower
Equisetum arvense	Horsetail
Foeniculum vulgare	Fennel
Hyssopus officinalis	Hyssop
Iris germanica florentina	Orris root, Florentine iris
Laurus nobilis	Sweet bay, bay tree, bay laurel
Lavandula angustifolia syn. *Lavandula officinalis*, *Lavandula vera*	Lavender
Levisticum officinale	Lovage
Lippia citriodora see *Aloysia triphylla*	
Lonicera periclymenum	Honeysuckle, woodbine
Melissa officinalis	Balm, lemon balm
Mentha pulegium decumbens	Pennyroyal
Mentha spicata	Garden, common or spearmint
Monarda didyma	Bergamot, Oswego tea, bee balm
Myrrhis odorata	Sweet cicely
Nepeta cataria	Catmint, catnip, catnep
Ocimum basilicum	Basil
Origanum majorana	Sweet marjoram
Pelargonium spp.	Scented-leaf geraniums
Petroselinum crispum	Parsley
Poterium sanguisorba	Burnet (salad)
Rosa gallica officinalis	Apothecary's rose, French rose, red damask rose, Provins rose
Rosmarinus officinalis	Rosemary
Rubia tinctorum	Madder
Rumex scutatus	French sorrel, buckler-leaved sorrel
Ruta graveolens	Rue, herb of grace
Salvia officinalis	Sage
Salvia sclarea	Clary
Sambucus nigra	Elder
Santolina chamaecyparissus	Cotton lavender, lavender cotton
Satureja hortensis	Summer savory
Satureja montana	Winter savory
Symphytum officinale	Comfrey, knitbone
Tanacetum vulgare	Tansy
Taraxacum officinale	Dandelion
Thymus vulgaris	Garden thyme
Trigonella foenum-graecum	Fenugreek
Urtica dioica	Stinging nettle
Valeriana officinalis	Valerian
Verbascum thapsus	Mullein
Verbena officinalis	Vervain

Cultivation

Name	Type	Soil	Site	Sow
ANGELICA	short-lived perennial	moist, deep, fertile	sun, light shade	late summer, early autumn
BALM, LEMON	herbaceous perennial	any average	sun or shade	spring, early autumn
BASIL, SWEET	half-hardy annual	fertile, well-drained	sun	early May
BAY, SWEET	shrub, tree	average, well-drained	sun, sheltered	
BERGAMOT	herbaceous perennial	moist, well-drained	sun	spring
BORAGE	hardy annual	any average	sun, light shade	spring-autumn
BURNET, SALAD	herbaceous perennial	chalky, well-drained	sun, sheltered	spring
CARAWAY	biennial	sandy, well-drained	sun	late spring
CATMINT	herbaceous	dryish, fertile, slightly alkaline	sun, light shade	late summer, spring
CHAMOMILE	herbaceous perennial	moist, fertile, well-drained	sun	
CHERVIL	hardy annual	moist	light shade	spring, late summer
CHIVES	bulb	light, moist	sun, light shade	spring, late summer
CLARY	biennial	any average	sun, shade	spring
COMFREY	herbaceous	deep, moist	sun, shade	
CORIANDER	hardy annual	light, well-drained	sun	spring
COSTMARY	herbaceous perennial	any average	sun	
COTTON LAVENDER	sub-shrub	light, well-drained	sun	
DANDELION	herbaceous perennial	any average	sun, shade	spring-autumn
DILL	hardy annual	moist, well-drained	sun	spring
ELDER	shrub, tree	any average, pref. moist	sun, light shade	late summer
FENNEL	herbaceous perennial	moist, chalky	sun, light shade	spring
FENUGREEK	half-hardy annual	fertile, well-drained	sun	late spring, protect at first
FEVERFEW	herbaceous perennial	any average	sun, shade	spring, summer
GARLIC	bulb	light, well-drained	sun, shelter	
GERANIUM, SCENTED-LEAVED	half-hardy perennial	light, well-drained	sun	
HONEYSUCKLE	shrub, climber	moist, fertile, alkaline	a little shade and sun	
HORSERADISH	herbaceous perennial	any average	sun, shade	
HORSETAIL	herbaceous perennial	any	sun, shade	
HYSSOP	sub-shrub	dry, well-drained	sun	spring
LAVENDER	shrub	alkaline, well-drained	sun, shelter	

Plant	Space	Thin	Prick out/ Container	Increase	Part used
transplant 6-12 months later	45 cm (18 in) thinned, 90 cm (3 ft) final	yes	no	seed, offsets	stem, seed; leaf/root occasionally
spring, autumn	45 cm (18 in)	yes	yes	seed, division	leaf
early June	30-45 cm (12-18 in)	yes	yes	seed	leaf
spring	only one required		yes	semi-hardwood cuttings	leaf
autumn, spring	45 cm (18 in)	yes	no	seed, division	leaf, flowering plant, root
	23-30 cm (9-12 in)	yes	yes	seed	leaf, flower
spring	15-23 cm (6-9 in)	yes	yes	seed, division	leaf
	30 cm (12 in)	yes	yes	seed	seed mainly, also leaf, root
spring	40 cm (16 in)	yes	yes	seed, division	leaf, flowering top
early spring	23 cm (9 in)		yes	runner division	flower
	23 cm (9 in)	yes	yes	seed	leaf
spring	15 cm (6 in)	yes	yes	seed, division	leaf
autumn	23 cm (9 in)	yes	yes	seed	leaf, seed
spring, autumn	60 cm (24 in)		no	division, root with bud	leaf, root, stem, flower
	20 cm (8 in)	yes	yes	seed	seed, leaf
spring, autumn	60 cm (24 in)		no	division	leaf
late spring	45-60 cm (18-24 in)		yes	heel cuttings	leaf, shoot
	15 cm (6 in)	yes	yes	seed, root cuttings	leaf, root, flower, stem
	23 cm (9 in)	yes	yes	seed	leaf, seed
autumn-spring	2.4 m (8 ft)+		no	seed, hardwood cuttings	flower, fruit, leaf, bark, root
spring	45 cm (18 in)	yes	yes, if deep	seed, division	leaf, seed; root, stem
	23 cm (9 in)	yes	yes	seed	seed, leaf
autumn	30 cm (12 in)	yes	yes	seed, division, heel cuttings	leaf, flower, whole plant
cloves, mid-spring, mid-autumn	15 cm (6 in)		yes	cloves	bulb
late spring	45 cm (18in)		yes	tip cuttings, spring, summer	leaf
autumn-spring	120 cm (4 ft)		yes, large, deep	hardwood cuttings autumn, layering	flower
early spring	45 cm (18 in)		yes	root cuttings, late winter	root
autumn			no	division	shoots
spring	30 cm (12 in)	yes	yes	seed, division, tip cuttings before flowering	leaf, flowering top
late spring	60 cm (24 in)		yes	heel cuttings spring, late summer	flower spikes

Name	Type	Soil	Site	Sow
LEMON VERBENA	tender shrub	light, well-drained	sun, shelter	
LOVAGE	herbaceous perennial	deep, moist, fertile	sun, light shade	spring
MADDER	climbing herbaceous perennial	deep, well-drained	light shade	spring, early summer
MARIGOLD	hardy annual	light, well-drained	sun	spring
MARJORAM, SWEET	half-hardy annual	moist, fertile	sun, shelter	end of late spring
MARSHMALLOW	herbaceous perennial	moist	sun, light shade	spring
MINT, GARDEN	herbaceous perennial	any average	sun, shade	spring
MULLEIN	biennial	well-drained	sun	early-midsummer
MUSTARD	hardy annual	moist, fertile	sun	spring
NETTLE	herbaceous perennial	any average	sun, shade	late summer, autumn, spring
ORRIS ROOT	rhizomatous perennial	dry, chalky, fertile, deep, well-drained	sun	
PARSLEY	biennial	deep, moist, fertile	sun, light shade	spring, midsummer
PENNYROYAL	herbaceous perennial	moist, fertile	sun, shade	late spring
PINK	herbaceous perennial	starved, well-drained	sun, shelter	mid-late spring
ROSE	shrub	moist, deep, fertile, well-drained	sun, light shade	
ROSEMARY	shrub	light, well-drained	sun, shelter	
RUE	sub-shrub	dry, poor	sun, shelter	mid-late spring
SAGE	sub-shrub	light, well-drained	sun, shelter	mid-spring
SAVORY, SUMMER	annual	dry, chalky, fertile	sun	spring
SAVORY, WINTER	sub-shrub	light, chalky, poor	sun	late summer, uncovered
SOUTHERNWOOD	sub-shrub	average to light	sun	
SWEET CICELY	herbaceous perennial	moist, deep, neutral-acid	sun, light shade	spring, late summer
SORREL	herbaceous perennial	moist, fertile, well-drained	sun, light shade	spring
TANSY	herbaceous perennial	any average	sun, light shade	spring, autumn
TARRAGON, FRENCH	herbaceous perennial	poor, well-drained	sun	
THYME	sub-shrub	poor, well-drained	sun, shelter	early summer
VALERIAN	herbaceous perennial	any average, moist	sun, light shade	spring, uncovered
VERVAIN	herbaceous	fertile, moist	sun	spring
WALLFLOWER	biennial	well-drained	sun	late spring, early summer
YARROW	hardy perennial	any average	sun	spring

Plant	Space	Thin	Prick out/ Container	Increase	Part used
late spring	average 120 cm (48 in)		yes, large	soft cuttings, midsummer	leaf
transplant autumn	120 cm (48 in)	yes	no	seed, root cuttings	leaf, seed, root, whole plant
spring, autumn	45 cm (18 in)	yes	no	seed, division	root
	25 cm (10 in)	yes	yes	seed	flower, leaf
early summer	20 cm (8 in)	yes	yes	seed	leaf, whole flowering plant
autumn	60 cm (24 in)	yes	no	seed, division	leaf, root, flower
autumn, spring	45 cm (18 in)	yes	yes	runner separation, seed seldom	leaf
transplant autumn	60 cm (24 in)	yes	yes	seed	leaf, flower, flower spikes
	30-45 cm (12-18 in)	yes	seedlings, yes	seed	seed, leaf
	38 cm (15 in)	yes	yes	seed, runners	leaf, stem, root
spring	38 cm (15 in)		yes, if deep	division July, early autumn	root
	20 cm (8 in)	yes	yes, if deep	seed	leaf, root
autumn, spring	15 cm (6 in)	yes	yes	seed, division	leaf, flowering plant
late summer	30 cm (12 in)	yes	yes	seed, layer, division	flower
autumn-spring	90 cm (36 in)		yes, if tub	hardwood cuttings	flower, fruit (hips)
late spring	90-150 cm (36-60 in)		yes	tip cuttings	leaf, flower
mid-late spring	30 cm (12 in)	yes	yes	seed, semi-hardwood cuttings	leaf
mid-late spring	45 cm (18 in)	yes	yes	seed, tip cuttings	leaf
	15 cm (6 in)	yes	yes	seed	leaf
spring	30 cm (12 in)	yes	yes	seed, division, layer	leaf
spring	60 cm (24 in)		yes	tip cuttings, heel cuttings	leaf, whole plant
spring, autumn	45 cm (18 in)	yes	no	seed, root division	leaf, root, seed
spring, autumn	38 cm (15 in)	yes	yes	seed, division	leaf
spring, autumn	45 cm (18 in)	yes	yes, if deep	seed, division	leaf, flower
late spring	60 cm (2 ft)		yes	division	leaf
spring	20 cm (8 in)	yes	yes	seed, layer, tip cuttings, division	leaf, flowering plant
spring, autumn	45 cm (18 in)	yes	no	seed, division	root
spring, autumn	38 cm (15 in)	yes	yes	seed, division	leaf, flowering plant
transplant mid-autumn	23 cm (9 in)	yes	yes	seed	flower
spring, autumn	30-60 cm (1-2 ft)		no	seed, division	leaf

Harvesting and drying

Name	Part Used	Stage/Time to Harvest
ANGELICA	leaf and flower stems, seed, leaf/root occasionally	stems when young and leaves May-June; roots autumn 1st year; seed when ripe August
BALM, LEMON	leaves	young, at any time; preferably just before flowering in dull, cool conditions
BASIL, SWEET	leaves	young, at any time for fresh use; just before flowering early morning when dry
BAY, SWEET	leaves	all year; for drying, early in the morning
BERGAMOT	leaves, flowers; root rarely	leaves at any time, just before flowering for drying; flowers at midsummer for drying; root in autumn
BORAGE	leaves, flowers	fresh leaves at any time, flowers from spring-autumn; use young leaves for drying
BURNET, SALAD	mainly fresh leaf; whole plant, dried root	fresh leaf at any time, root for drying early autumn
CARAWAY	seeds; leaves and root occasionally	when ripe, July-August; cut seedheads just as first seeds fall
CATMINT	leaves, flowering plant	fresh leaves at any time, flowers in full bloom July-August; leaves for drying just before flowering starts
CHAMOMILE	flowers	when fully open, in dry, sunny conditions, by hand, with no stem, throughout summer
CHERVIL	mainly fresh leaf; also whole plant and dried root	fresh leaf at any time, root for drying early autumn
CHIVES	leaves	throughout growing season
CLARY	seed, leaves	young leaves for drying, otherwise at any time; seed when ripe midsummer
COMFREY	leaves, root	fresh leaves at any time, roots in autumn
CORIANDER	seeds, leaves	seed just as first begin to fall and aroma becomes pleasant; fresh leaf at any time, for drying
COSTMARY	leaves	fresh at any time; for drying cut just before flowering, when dry, early in day
COTTON LAVENDER	leaves	fresh, at any time; for drying, in early summer
DANDELION	root, leaf; flower rarely	fresh leaves at any time, and also for drying
DILL	leaf, seed	fresh leaves at any time; for drying just after flowering; seed in late summer as it starts to turn brown
ELDER	flowers, fruits, leaves, stems, roots	flowers early-midsummer; fruit late summer-early autumn; remainder at any time except leaves, which gather early-midsummer
FENNEL	leaf	fresh leaves at any time; for drying, usually not satisfactory by home methods
FENUGREEK	seed, leaves	leaf from early summer, seed from late summer
FEVERFEW	leaves, flowering tops	fresh leaf at any time, for drying, just before flowering midsummer-mid-autumn
GARLIC	cloves	mid-late summer when leaves have yellowed
GERANIUM, SCENTED-LEAVED	leaves	spring-early autumn
HONEYSUCKLE	flowers	just as they open fully, early summer-early autumn, when dry
HORSERADISH	root	any time from plants up to two years old, from the thicker parts
HORSETAIL	shoots	early-late summer, using barren green shoots
HYSSOP	leaves, flowering tops	fresh leaves at any time; leaves for drying just before flowering, at mid-summer
LAVENDER	flowers	just as the flowers come into full bloom, July-August

Method of Drying/Preserving	Remarks
dry leaves with good ventilation; clean roots and dry quickly	do not allow to flower if leaves wanted
dry quickly at higher temperatures with plenty of air	use fresh or dry
always in dark, dry quickly at higher temperatures, but not above 30°C	leaves bruise easily and thus lose oils; use fresh or dry; dry as quickly as possible after harvesting; remove flowerheads before opening
dry at the lower temperatures to retain colour and press afterwards as they will have curled up	generally used dried, but can be used fresh, then remove earlier from dish
dry leaves and flowers by standard method (see p. 116)	use fresh or dried flowers or leaves for tea
dry leaves quickly, with good ventilation, at low temperature, always in the dark	difficult to dry as it readily discolours and loses its essential oils; use flowers fresh for candying
nearly evergreen, need not be dried; best flavour fresh; root by standard method	mostly used fresh in salads
hang seedheads over tray in dry, airy, dark place or place in paper bags	leaves and root used fresh
dry leaves quickly, with good ventilation, at low temperature; dry flowers by standard method (see p. 116)	
dry quickly, with good ventilation	touch as little as possible at any time
advisable not to dry chervil, as it is very difficult to retain delicate flavour, and thin leaves reduce considerably; root by standard method or freeze	fresh chervil available all year, if sown in autumn as well as spring
not usually dried as difficult to retain mild flavour	can be quick-frozen for winter use
dry leaves quickly, with good ventilation, at low temperatures, in dark	
dry roots by standard method (see p. 116), will take about a week and should snap cleanly	use leaves fresh, roots fresh or dried and powdered
hang seedheads to dry in paper bags, head downwards	leaves always used fresh
dry by standard method (see p. 116)	easily become brittle
dry leaves on stem, as complete shoots; ventilate well	touch as little as possible
dry leaves and roots by standard method (see p. 116), roots take about 2 weeks	split up larger roots for quicker drying, inside will be white when dry; they lose 76% of their weight
great care needed with fine leaves; handle gently, and keep temperatures lower rather than at maximum, ventilate well; seed can be dried without extra heat	seed can be used instead of leaves to supply characteristic flavour
handle flowers carefully and little; spread out and ventilate well, dry by standard method, also leaves	
	leaves last until late autumn-early winter in mild areas
normally used fresh, but standard method may be tried if dried leaves required	
by standard method	bitter flavour may need to be masked
dig up bulbs complete and dry in warmth on hard, dry surface 3-4 days, protected from sun, then hang in dry, well-ventilated place	
handle gently, as little as possible, dry quickly but not with high temperatures	leaf colour is easily lost in drying process
for dry potpourri by standard method, and always in dark to retain colour; for moist potpourri, part dry until flabby	use whole flower including stamens
horseradish root always used fresh	
dry whole, do not break up, handle as little as possible, use standard method	do not break up until just before use
use standard method	
cut with stems about 20 cm (8 in) long, hang upside down in dark, airy place, warm, and in bags to protect from dust	remove gently from stems to avoid loss of aroma too soon

Name	Part Used	Stage/Time to Harvest
LEMON VERBENA	leaves	fresh leaves at any time; for drying in late summer as flowering is about to start
LOVAGE	leaves, seed, root, whole plant	young outer leaves, not heart leaves, for drying; fresh leaves at any time with same proviso; seed in late summer; root in spring or autumn
MADDER	root	best in autumn
MARIGOLD	petals	in just full bloom, in summer
MARJORAM, SWEET	leaves	from early summer to end of growing season; for drying, just as buds about to show flowers
MARSHMALLOW	leaf, root, flower	root should be two years old; leaves taken just as flowering starts, leave fresh or dried
MINT, GARDEN	leaves	fresh at any time from late spring; for drying, just as first flowers appear, early morning or evening
MULLEIN	leaf, flower, flower-spike	flowers fresh early-late summer, in early morning when dry; leaves before flowering or after
MUSTARD	seed, seedling	seed late summer, seedling a few days after germination
NETTLE, STINGING	leaf, shoots	young leaves and shoots at any time, for fresh or dried use
ORRIS ROOT	rhizome	dig up two-year-old rhizomes in autumn
PARSLEY	leaves	for fresh use at any time; during summer for drying
PENNYROYAL	leaves	fresh at any time; for drying just at flowering time in late summer
PINK	flower	just in full flower, midsummer, early on dry day
ROSE	flower, fruit (hips)	flowers when in full bloom, early morning on dry day; red hips in early autumn
ROSEMARY	leaves, flower	at any time of year for fresh use; just before flowering in mid-late spring for drying
RUE	leaves, shoots	before flowering, any time in spring, midsummer
SAGE	leaves	at any time up to flowering; from new shoots growing after flowering; for drying, in second and subsequent years, a few days before flowering
SAVORY, SUMMER	leaves	fresh leaves from early summer to mid-autumn; for drying just after flowering starts
SAVORY, WINTER	leaves	fresh leaves from second-year plants, late spring onwards
SOUTHERNWOOD	leaves, whole plant	for drying, any time until just before flowering late summer
SWEET CICELY	leaves, seed, root	fresh leaves from mid-spring until late autumn; for drying in very early summer, or just before flowering; seed when dark brown to black and about to fall; root dug in autumn and following of second year, used fresh
SORREL	leaves	fresh leaves and for drying at any time from spring to autumn
TANSY	leaf, shoots	fresh leaves when young; for drying just before flowering, early in late summer, also shoots at this time
TARRAGON	leaves	fresh leaves from early summer to mid-autumn; for drying early in midsummer
THYME	leaves	at any time, preferably before/at flowering in midsummer if to be dried
VALERIAN	root	in the second year, in late autumn
VERVAIN	leaf, flowering plant	fresh leaves at any time; for drying before flowering in midsummer; whole plant in midsummer
WALLFLOWER	flowers	just as they are fully open, mid-late spring, early morning on dry day
YARROW	leaves, stems, flowers	fresh leaves at any time, flowers just as they open, stems with them, leaves for drying just before flower buds unfold

Method of Drying/Preserving	Remarks
with same care as for scented-leaved geranium	
use low temperature and dry leaves moderately quickly; whole plant will take some time because of stout stems	prevent flowering if leaves only wanted; seeds will provide same flavour
use standard method	can be used fresh, cut into pieces
pull singly from flower, and dry in complete dark, in thin layers, with plenty of ventilation	can be used fresh
darkness important, high rather than low temperature, single layers of leaves	aroma stronger when dried
by standard method; may take longer than usual due to thickness of root and leaves	
handle carefully and little as leaves easily blacken; ventilate well	prevent plant from flowering; strip leaves from stems after drying and rub; peppermint for tea should be left whole
always dry flowers without light, immediately after collecting, do not bruise, use standard method otherwise	any loss of yellow colour makes flowers useless
seed allowed to ripen naturally, and kept in airtight, lightproof containers	mustard is replaced by rape in the salad mustard and cress
by standard method	sting is removed by drying
by standard method	violet perfume increases with age of dried rhizome
dry quickly at high rather than low temperature, with good ventilation, to retain green colour	must be kept really dark and airtight for good colour and aroma; can be quick-frozen
by standard method	nearly evergreen, so fresh leaves readily available
by standard method for dry potpourri; or dry only till limp for moist mixtures	use fresh petals with white 'heels' cut off for food and drink flavouring
flowers as for pink, but keep quite dark at all times to ensure best colour	hips mostly used fresh
evergreen, need not be dried, but if necessary, by standard method fairly quickly, with plenty of air; flowers with lower temperature	
by standard method, dry thin leaves quickly	remove flowering tops if maximum leaves wanted
care needed as they lose colour easily at high temperature, but take long time at low temperature; spread out very thinly	
by standard method	dry sprigs rather than individual leaves
evergreen except in severe winters	does not dry well
by standard method with plenty of ventilation	dry whole shoots or tips of shoots, then remove leaves
leaves do not dry successfully; seed will provide same flavour, and can be spread out on tray to dry	plant often produces leaves from late winter until late autumn
with plenty of ventilation for succulent leaves; handle little to avoid bruising	mostly used fresh; take only small quantities from young plants; prevent flowering
by standard method	
dry sprigs and shoots to avoid handling leaves which bruise very easily and turn black; use low temperature, and keep quite dark	can be quick-frozen or preserved in oil
by standard method, as sprigs or shoots	thyme is evergreen
clean thoroughly with strong spray, and split thicker roots into half or quarters; make sure they are thoroughly dry	
by standard method; use sprigs of leaves	
in complete darkness, on the flowering stems	can be used for dry or moist potpourri
by standard method of drying	stems and flowers may take longer than usual

Herbal recipes

BORAGE

Borage with cream cheese
Borage leaves give a light cucumber flavour to a bland cream or cottage cheese.
100g/4oz/¹/₄lb cream cheese or cottage cheese
1 tbls finely chopped borage leaves
lemon juice
Blend the cream cheese and borage leaves together until they are thoroughly mixed. If desired, add a little lemon juice for flavouring and serve on crackers or bread. In larger quantities, this can be served as a party dip.

CARAWAY

Victorian seed cake
300g/12oz/1¹/₂ cups butter
300g/12oz/1¹/₂ cups castor sugar
400g/1lb flour
6 eggs
milk
grated nutmeg, powdered mace and caraway seeds, all to taste
Beat the butter until thickly creamy and beat in the sugar and spices well. Whisk each egg separately and beat them in one at a time, beating well between each. Then fold in the flour together with a little milk to bring it to a dropping consistency. Bake for 1¹/₂-2 hours at 180°C/350°F/Gas Mark 4 using a 20cm (8in) cake tin (non-stick or greased and lined with greaseproof paper).

CORIANDER

Ratatouille with coriander
This can be served hot or cold.
2 large onions
2 aubergines
1 green pepper
1 red pepper
200g/8oz/¹/₂lb courgettes
200g/8oz/¹/₂lb skinned tomatoes
2 cloves of garlic
2 tbls ground coriander seeds
3 tbls olive oil
salt and freshly ground pepper
Cut the aubergines into cubes, sprinkle with salt and leave to drain, in a colander for 20 minutes. Slice the onions and cook them gently in a heavy bottomed saucepan with the oil. Seed and chop the peppers, slice the courgettes and chop the skinned tomatoes. When the onions are soft, add peppers and aubergines and simmer gently for about 20 minutes, adding a little more oil if necessary. Then add the tomatoes, garlic, courgettes and ground coriander and cook for another 15-20 minutes until all the vegetables are soft but not mushy. Add salt and pepper to taste and serve, or transfer to a bowl and allow to cool.

DILL

Dill sauce
A delicious sauce to serve with boiled meats, chicken, fish and game. It can also be served with eggs and cooked vegetables such as cabbage and potatoes.
25g/1oz/2 tbls butter
1 tbls flour
300ml/¹/₂ pint/1¹/₄ cups stock
150ml/¹/₄ pint/²/₃ cup sour cream
3 tbls chopped dill (or in winter 1) teaspoon crushed seeds)
1 teaspoon French mustard
salt and freshly ground black pepper
Melt the butter in a saucepan, add the flour and cook for 2 minutes, stirring all the time. Heat the stock and the sour cream together and blend into the butter and flour mixture. Simmer gently for about 6-8 minutes. Add the mustard and salt and pepper to taste, then stir in the chopped dill just before serving.

ELDER

Elderflower sorbet
6-8 fresh elderflower heads (or 2 tbls dried)
900ml/1¹/₂ pints/3³/₄ cups water
150 g/6oz/³/₄ cup sugar
juice and rind of 4 lemons
Slowly heat the water and sugar in a saucepan until the syrup is clear. Remove from the heat and add the flowers, lemon juice and rind and steep for about 1 hour. Strain into metal trays and freeze. Remove the stiff mixture 2 or 3 times from the freezer and whip well to break up the ice crystals. Serve when the mixture is a firm mush.

GARLIC

Garlic bread
1 French loaf
2-3 cloves of garlic (depending on size)
75g/3oz/6tbls butter, slightly softened
Peel and crush the garlic with mortar and pestle or a garlic crusher and work into the butter until it is evenly distributed. Make wide diagonal cuts on the loaf, stopping just before you cut right through it. Spread the butter on each side of the sliced bread, close up the loaf and spread any remaining butter over the crust. Wrap in kitchen foil and bake in a fairly hot oven (190°C/375°F/Gas mark 5) for about 15 minutes.

SCENTED-LEAVED GERANIUMS

Scented blackberries
Sweet-scented geraniums have a remarkable affinity with blackberries and give them a most attractive flavour.
400g/1lb blackberries
150ml/¹/₄ pint/²/₃ cup water
100g/4oz/¹/₄ lb sugar
2 scented geranium leaves
Make a syrup by boiling the sugar and water together for 6 to 8 minutes with the geranium leaves. Drop in the blackberries and cook briefly until tender. Allow to cool, then chill in the refrigerator for several hours. Remove the geranium leaves before serving with whipped or clotted cream.

MARJORAM

Marjoram soda bread
200g/8oz/2 cups self-raising flour
³/₄ teaspoon dried marjoram (basil or thyme can be substituted)
2 tbls sugar
1 teaspoon salt
1 egg
5 tbls milk
12g/¹/₂oz/1 tbls melted butter
Mix dry ingredients thoroughly in a bowl. Beat the egg, butter and milk together and add to the dry mixture. Knead lightly on a floured board and put into a buttered cake tin. Bake in a hot oven, 200°C/400°F/Gas Mark 6, for about 45 minutes. This is best eaten hot, or as soon as possible after removing from the oven; soda bread becomes hard and stale quite quickly.

PARSLEY

Moules marinière with parsley
2kg/4lbs mussels
2 chopped onions
2 cloves of garlic, finely chopped
2 tbls chopped parsley
300ml/¹/₂ pint/1¹/₄ cups dry white wine
50g/2oz/¹/₄ cup butter
salt and freshly ground pepper
Scrub and beard the mussels under cold running water. Put the onions, garlic, wine and 1 tbls parsley in a large saucepan. Boil for about 5 minutes before adding the mussels. Then cover the pan and cook over high heat for about 5-8 minutes, shaking the pan constantly. When all the mussels have opened, remove them to a deep dish. Strain the mussel juice, return to the saucepan, add the butter and heat through before pouring over mussels. Sprinkle with remaining parsley.

Salsa verde
In Italy, this sauce is traditionally served with *bollito misto* (mixed boiled meats), but it also makes an excellent accompaniment to poached white fish, artichokes, asparagus and many other vegetables.
3 tbls chopped parsley (or parsley, dill and tarragon mixed)
2 tbls finely chopped capers
6 anchovy fillets mashed to a paste (or 1 tbls anchovy essence)
1 clove garlic crushed
¹/₂ teaspoon Dijon mustard
1 teaspoon wine vinegar (or 1 tbls lemon juice)
8 tbls olive oil
Put herbs, capers, mashed anchovy, garlic and mustard in a bowl and mix well. Add the vinegar or lemon juice and then the olive oil, beating it in so it is well amalgamated. This sauce will keep for a week in the refrigerator but needs to be thoroughly mixed again before serving.

ROSE

Rose hip syrup
Rose hips are a rich source of vitamin C and this sweet, fruity syrup is popular with children either served on ice-cream and other puddings, or topped up with sparkling mineral water to make a pleasant fizzy drink.
300ml/¹/₂ pint/1¹/₄ cups boiling water
100g/4oz/¹/₄lb rose hips
100g/4oz/¹/₂ cup sugar
Pour boiling water over the rose hips, cover and leave to get cold. Strain the infusion, add the sugar and bring slowly to the boil. Simmer gently until syrupy. Cool and pour into a sterilized jar or bottle.

Rose water (skin freshener, hair rinse for greasy hair)
In Middle Eastern and Indian cooking rose water is often used to flavour food. In India it is added to ice-cream and cakes and in many Arab countries it is used as a glaze for roasting chicken.
200g/8oz/¹/₂lb rose petals
approx 300ml/¹/₂ pint/1¹/₄ cups rain, spring or distilled water
Put the freshly-picked rose petals into an enamel saucepan with just enough water to cover the petals. Bring to the boil and simmer gently for about 30 minutes. Strain and discard the rose petals. When cool, pour into sterilized jars and leave for 3 days before using.

ROSEMARY

Roast lamb with rosemary
This is one of the simplest and most delicious ways to cook lamb.
1 leg or shoulder of lamb
2-3 sprigs rosemary
2-3 cloves garlic
olive oil
salt and freshly ground pepper
Make several incisions in a leg or shoulder of lamb. Cut the cloves of garlic in half and insert along with sprigs of rosemary broken in half. Rub the meat with olive oil and salt and pepper, and roast in the usual way. Add some potatoes half way through the cooking so that they can absorb the rosemary and garlic meat juices.

TARRAGON

Tarragon chicken
A classic dish, best made in summer when fresh tarragon is available.
1.5-1.75kg/3¹/₂-4lb roasting chicken
3 tbls chopped, fresh tarragon
100g/4oz/¹/₂ cup butter
150ml/¹/₄ pint/²/₃ cup cream
1 tbls flour
salt and pepper to taste
oil for cooking
Mix 2 tbls chopped tarragon with half the butter, season with salt and pepper and stuff the chicken with this mixture. Melt the rest of the butter with a little oil in a flameproof casserole, add the chicken, cover

tightly and slowly on top of the cooker or in a moderate oven, 180°C/350°F/Gas Mark 4, for 1½-2 hours or until the chicken is tender. During the cooking, baste the chicken frequently with the tarragon-flavoured butter and if necessary, add a little water or stock to prevent the chicken from burning. When the chicken is done, remove it to a serving dish and keep warm. Add the flour to the juices in the casserole, stir well and cook for about 2 minutes, then add the cream and the remainder of the chopped tarragon. Bring to the boil and simmer for a couple of minutes before pouring the sauce over the chicken.

YARROW

Yarrow infusion (for minor cuts and wounds)
Yarrow leaves can be directly applied to cuts and wounds as a poultice. Drop the leaves in boiling water for a few seconds, then cool before using on affected part. Alternatively, make a yarrow infusion to bathe cuts and wounds.
1 large handful of yarrow leaves
600ml/1 pint/2½ cups boiling water
Pour the boiling water over slightly bruised leaves and leave to get cool. Strain the liquid into a bowl, soak gauze dressing in the infusion and apply to cuts, grazes or wounds.

Yarrow face pack (for greasy skin and spots)
1 egg white
1 teaspoon lemon juice
2 tbls finely chopped yarrow leaves
Mix the ingredients together, blending well. Spread the mixture over the face, avoiding the eyes and mouth, and leave for about 10-15 minutes. Rinse off with lukewarm water.

Herb suppliers & useful addresses

Ashfields Herb Nursery
Hinstock
Market Drayton
Salop TF9 2NG
plants and seeds

Herbs from the Hoo
46 Church Street
Bucken
Huntingdon
Cambs PE18 9SX
plants

The Herb Centre
Thornby Hall Gardens
Thornby
Northampton NN6 8SW

Hollington Nurseries Ltd.
Woolton Hill
Newbury
Berks.
plants

Norfolk Lavender Ltd.
Caley Mill
Heacham
King's Lynn
Norfolk PE31 7JE

Oak Cottage
Herb Farm
Nesscliffe
Salop SY4 1DB
plants

Poyntzfield Nursery Garden
by Dingwall
Black Isle
Ross-shire, Scotland
plants

Samares Herbs a Plenty
Samares Manor
St Clement
Jersey, C.I.

Stoke Lacy Herb Farm
Bromyard
Hereford HR4 7JH
plants

Suffolk Herbs
Sawyers Farm
Little Cornard
Sudbury
Suffolk
seeds

The Old Rectory Herb Garden
Rectory Lane
Ightham
Kent TN15 9AL

Thornham Herbs
The Walled Garden
Thornham Magna
Eye, Suffolk
plants

Valeswood Herb Farm
Little Ness
Shrewsbury
Salop
plants

Yorkshire Herbs
The Herb Centre
Middleton Tyas
Richmond, Yorks
plants

Herb *seed* can also be obtained from the leading general seedsmen, such as:

J. W. Boyce
67 Station Road
Soham
Ely
Cambs CB7 5ED

Thomas Butcher Ltd.
60 Wickham Road
Shirley
Croydon
Surrey CR9 8AG

Chase Organics Ltd.
Seed Division
Gibraltar House
Shepperton
Middx TW17 8AQ

Samuel Dobie & Son Ltd.
Upper Dee Mills
Llangollen
Clwyd LL20 8SD

S. E. Marshall & Co. Ltd.
Regal Road
Wisbech
Cambs PE13 2RF

Thompson & Morgan
London Road
Ipswich
Suffolk IP2 0BA

Sutton & Sons Ltd.
Hele Road
Torquay
Devon TQ2 7QJ

Unwins Seeds Ltd.
Histon
Cambs CB4 4LE

American Museum
Claverton Manor
Bath
Avon BA2 7BD

Barnsley House Gardens
Barnsley, Cirencester
Glos

Beaulieu Abbey Cloisters
Beaulieu
Exbury
Hants

Butser Ancient Farm Research Project
Rookham Lodge
East Meon
Hants

Cambridge Botanic Garden
Cambs

Capel Manor Institute of Horticulture
Bullsmoor Lane
Waltham Cross
Herts EN7 5HR

Chelsea Physic Garden
66 Royal Hospital Rd
London SW3

County Demonstration Garden
Probus
Cornwall

Edinburgh Botanic Gardens
Edinburgh
Scotland

Hatfield House
Hatfield
Herts

The Herb Garden
The Queen's House
Kew Gardens
Kew
Richmond
Surrey

Lullingstone Castle
Lullingstone
Kent

Royal Horticultural Society's Garden
Wisley
Woking
Surrey

St Fagan's Garden
Cardiff
S. Wales

Spring Hill
County Londonderry
N. Ireland

Sissinghurst Castle Gardens
Sissinghurst
Cranbrook
Kent TN17 2AB

Withersdane Hall
Wye
Ashford
Kent

Times of opening can be obtained on application to the garden concerned.

The **Herb Society** is a national society with a growing international membership which publishes a quarterly journal, runs lectures and symposia, has a library and publishes its own books, and supplies and disseminates information on herbs.
Address is:
77 Great Peter St
London SW1
tel. 01-222 3634
Application for membership should be made to the Secretary at the above address.

Herbal medical courses are provided by the National Institute of Medical Herbalists at the
School of Herbal Medicine
Tunbridge Wells
Kent

Other **general interest courses** covering a wide range of herbal subjects are often run by the specialist herb nurseries, and usually last for a day or a weekend; the Herbal Weekend run at the Earnley Concourse, near Chichester, W. Sussex, is an annual event.
For details of courses around Britain, apply to the Herb Society.

Herbal products can be obtained from health food shops, some of the specialist herb nurseries, and from the Culpeper shops. The addresses of some specialist retail outlets are as follows:

Culpeper
 21 Bruton Street
 Berkeley Square
 London W1X 7DA

 9 Flask Walk
 Hampstead
 London NW3

 Addresses of their other shops may be obtained from their London branches

Cambridge Herb Company
Dry Drayton
Cambridge CB3 8AT

Chalk Farm Nutrition Centre
41-42 Chalk Farm Road
London NW1

Cranks Grain Shop
8 Marshall Street
off Carnaby Street
London W1

Dorwest Herb Growers
Shipton Gorge
Bridport
Dorset

L'Herbier de Provence
341 Fulham Road
London SW10

Meadow Herbs Ltd.
47 Moreton Street
Pimlico
London SW1
(*potpourri materials*)

Potters (Herbal Supplies) Ltd.
Leyland Mill Lane
Wigan

York Perfumery
29 Goodramgate
York
Yorks

For those with **commercial interests** in herbs, there is a British Herb Trades Association, and the address of the Director is:
Mr R. Peplow
Herbs from the Hoo
46 Church Street
Buckden
Huntingdon
Cambs PE18 9SX

A herbal holiday is run by:
Heches Herbs of Guernsey
Les Heches
St Peter in the Wood
Guernsey
Channel Islands
lasting approximately a week; the Course Director will provide further details.

AUSTRALIA

NSW

Beaufort Herbs
Beaufort
Cootamundra, NSW

Father Pierre's Monastery Herbs
169 Coxs Road
North Ryde, Sydney

Kadisna Herb Farm & Nursery
113 Bells Line of Road
Kurrajong Heights, NSW

Somerset Cottage Herb Garden & Shop
745 Old Northern Road
Dural, Sydney

Tasslex Aromatic Herbs
198 Pacific Highway
Lindfield, Sydney

Victoria

Canna Brae Herb Garden
35 Felix Crescent
Ringwood North, Melbourne

City Herb Garden
120 Arnold Street
Carlton North, Melbourne

Herbs for Health
228 Settlement Road
Cowes, Vic.

Lilydale Herb Farm
61 Mangans Road
Lilydale, Melbourne

Wesburn Nursery
93 Warburton Highway
Wesburn, Vic.

Queensland

Chamomile Herb Farm
Long Road
Eagle Heights, Brisbane

Gift of Herbs
314 Oxley Road
Graceville, Brisbane

Happy Herb Centre
Logan River Road
Waterford, Brisbane

South Australia

Australerba
27 Blight Road
Ridleyton SA 5008

Calluna Croft Herb Nursery
Vine Vale Road
Tanunda SA 5352

Earthcraft Nurseries
1062 Lower North East Road
Highbury SA 5089

Hahndorf Herbs
17a Main Hahndorf
Hahndorf SA 5245

Hills Herbs
469 Mount Barker Road
Bridgewater SA 5155

Western Australia

Alpine Nursery
150 Armadale Road
Riverdale WA 6103

Maylands Garden Centre
43c Caledonian Avenue
Maylands WA 6051

Permaganic Growers
Strachan Road
Bullsbrook WA 6084

NEW ZEALAND

Herb suppliers

Kings Herbs
1660 Great North Road
Avondale, Auckland

The Herb Farm
Rue Grehan
Akaroa, Canterbury

Herb gardens to visit

Botanic Gardens in Auckland, Wellington and Dunedin and at Mona Vale in Christchurch

NZ Herb Societies (for complete list of herb nurseries and also public and private gardens which may be visited)

Auckland Herb Society
PO Box 20,022
Glen Eden, Auckland 7

Wellington Herb Society
PO Box 10,318
The Terrace, Wellington

Otago Herb Society
PO Box 5078
Dunedin, Otago

Glossary

Abortifacient: causing abortion.

Alternate: of leaves, growing singly up a stem, unlike leaves in pairs which occur opposite each other.

Annual: plant which flowers and sets seed once before dying, in a year or less.

Antiseptic: substance that can destroy infection-causing bacteria.

Astringent: substance that causes tissues to contract and prevents the secretion or discharge of fluids.

Biennial: plant which flowers in its second summer and then dies.

Blanch: in gardening, to exclude light from a plant to prevent its foliage from turning green; in cookery, to boil for a few minutes before draining and proceeding to cook as specified.

Colic: medical condition characterized by pain and flatulence of the abdomen.

Corolla: petals of a flower.

Culpeper, Nicholas: (1616-1654), doctor and apothecary who based his medical belief and practice on astrology. He lived at Spitalfields in London and believed that all plants, including what we now call medicinal herbs, were influenced by the planets; each had its own planet just as each illness or injury had its own planet. Cure, in effect, was simply a case of matching planets. He was a Puritan, fought and was wounded in the Civil War and died when he was 38, leaving a wife and seven children. A modern edition of his herbal remedies is in print, with illustrations.

Decoction: solution obtained by using the hard parts of plants and boiling them in water. With such tougher parts, it is only possible to obtain the required constituents by boiling. A true decoction is obtained by adding 25 g/1 oz of the plant part to 600 ml/1 pint/2½ cups of water, leaving it to soak for 10 minutes, then heating to boiling point and simmering for 10 to 15 minutes, then leaving to soak for another 10 minutes. The container should be covered throughout. The solution is strained and cooled and a cupful taken three times a day as an average dose.

Demulcent: softening or soothing agent taken internally to soothe membranes, or applied externally to irritations and inflamed or painful areas.

Diaphoretic: substance which increases perspiration, often used in the treatment of fevers.

Digestive: preparation or substance which increases the secretion of gastric juices and helps the process of food digestion.

Dioscorides: (1st century A.D.) Greek physician, contemporaneous with Pliny the Elder, born in Asia Minor and best known for writing a herbal, originally in Greek but now known under its Latin name, *De Materia Medica*. A magnificently illustrated copy of this was made in A.D. 512 which has survived and is now known as the *Codex Vindobonensis*. Forty-four of the drugs mentioned are still listed in modern official pharmacopoeias, having been continuously listed in translations of the work since its first appearance.

Distillation: process by which a substance is separated from another by boiling or steaming. For herbal oil extraction, the tougher parts such as roots or stems are placed in water and boiled steadily for some hours. The steam given off is collected in another container, the condenser, where it cools and the essential oil of the herb separates out from the water and can be skimmed off.

Diuretic: substance which increases the quantity of urine, and therefore stimulates its flow.

Division: method of plant increase by which plants are cut or chopped in half, or into more parts, at the crown. Herbaceous perennials which are particularly tough can be conveniently separated with two forks placed back to back in the centre of the crown and then forced apart.

Dyspepsia: indigestion.

Emollient: substance which soothes and softens the skin.

Enfleurage: method of extracting plant oil by using purified fat to absorb the plant or flower oil until it is saturated and becomes a 'pomade'. The essential oils are then extracted with an alcoholic solvent.

Expectorant: substance which loosens phlegm and helps to clear the bronchial tubes.

Expression: method of obtaining the essential oils from plants, usually applied to fruit. It involves subjecting the fruit to considerable pressure, as for instance that obtained in a cider press.

Extraction: another method of extracting plant oil, by using a solvent such as alcohol or petroleum ether. The solvent is run through the plant material continuously, being collected in a still. The resultant liquid is then distilled and a solid material will remain which is a mixture of waxes and essential oils.

Flatulence: condition caused by gas in the stomach or bowels.

Fumigant: substance which disinfects, or destroys pests.

Gerard, John: (1545-1612) surgeon and later apothecary to James I. He wrote a famous herbal, published in 1597, called the *Herball or Historie of Plantes*, which was largely based on a translation of another book by a Belgian botanist-doctor called Rembert Dodoens. Gerard's physic garden near Lincoln's Inn Fields in Holborn, London, contained many New World plant species brought to England by the 16th-century explorers and navigators.

Hippocrates: (c. 460-377 B.C.) ancient Greek physician regarded as the father of scientific medicine, largely because he rejected the supernatural as a cause of disease and insisted it resulted from an imbalance in the bodily humours. He used about 400 medicines, most of them derived from plants.

Inflorescence: flowerheads of a plant.

Infusion: solution made by pouring boiling water on to leaves, flowers, soft stems and other soft parts of plants, and leaving it to stand for a given time while the water soluble substances are extracted from them. Pour 600 ml/1 pint/2½ cups of boiling water on to 25 g/1 oz of the material, contained in a ceramic, stainless steel, glass, stone or enamel pan, fit with a tight lid and leave to infuse for 10 to 15 minutes. The solution is then strained and when tepid or cold, taken as directed.

Lanceolate: of leaves, narrow and gradually tapering at each end.

Layering: method of plant increase; a slanting cut is made partially through the underside of a new season's stem opposite a leaf joint. The stem chosen should be close to soil level, as the stem is then pegged down on to the soil, the cut being held open with a matchstick so that it is in contact with the soil, and the tip of the shoot trained straight up and supported with a small cane. The stem is covered with fine soil in the region of the cut where roots will form and a new plantlet will appear. The parent stem can be cut when the plantlet is well-rooted, but the plantlet should be left until the spring, or at any rate for some months, before planting in its permanent place. Layering can be done in spring and summer.

Laxative: substance that helps to promote bowel movement.

Maceration: the softening and separating of parts by steeping; of plants, the soaking of the soft parts in a solvent such as water to release the essential oils.

Mordant: a chemical such as alum, cream of tartar, chrome, iron or tin, used to 'fix' vegetable dyes so that they remain colour-fast.

Mucilage: a viscous, mucous-like substance produced by certain plants.

Mulch: layer of material on the soil around a plant, used to conserve water, prevent weed growth and provide a cool root run. If rotted organic matter is used, it will supply plant nutrient gradually and maintain a good soil structure.

Opposite: of leaves which grow in pairs, one opposite to the other up a stem.

Ovate: basically an egg-shaped leaf but the tip is tapering or pointed, and the end nearest the stem is the widest part of the leaf.

Pappus: feathery part of a seed as in dandelion 'clocks'.

Pea-flower: distinctive flower of the *Leguminosae* or pea plant family. It consists of five petals: the standard, upper, upright one being the largest; the two lateral ones or wings below it; and the two lowest, more or less fused together forming the keel.

Perennial, herbaceous: plant with soft tissues, not woody or covered with bark, that lives from year to year. The top growth often dies down completely in winter to ground level but the rootstocks remain alive, though dormant.

Pharynx: cavity behind nose, mouth and larynx which forms the upper part of the gullet.

Pinnate: of leaves, each consisting of pairs of leaflets along a central stem resembling a feather; doubly pinnate refers to leaflets which are divided in their turn in a similar arrangement.

Pliny the Elder: (A.D. 23-79) Roman civil servant, chiefly renowned for writing a vast *Natural History* in 37 books consisting of the accumulated knowledge of his times. He died going to the help of friends in the eruption of Vesuvius.

Pomade: a scented grease obtained by spreading fat, such as lard, evenly and thinly over the surface of both sides of a sheet of glass held in a frame. The flowers containing the desired perfume are spread over these surfaces and the glass plates stacked in the dark for a day and a night. The process is repeated daily with fresh flowers for several weeks, after which the fat will have absorbed the perfumed oils. See also *enfleurage*.

Prick out: to plant out seedlings from their germinating container into a larger one in which they are spaced out, usually about 5 cm (2 in) each way, to allow unrestricted growth. The seedlings should be held by a leaf and inserted up to the base of the seed leaves, so that the whole stem is within the planting hole and the leaves just above soil level.

Purgative: a strong laxative given to relieve constipation.

Rhizome: creeping underground stem from which shoots are sent up; it is often thick and acts as a food storage organ.

Sedative: a medicine which calms the nerves.

Semi-hardwood (half-ripe): of cuttings, made from stems, they are shoots produced in the current season using the top or end 7-15 cm (3-6 in). The stem will have begun to turn brown and become tough at its base, but the tip will still be soft and green. Such cuttings are usually made in July and August.

Soft: of stem cuttings, referring to the tip part of a stem whose tissue is still tender, and sometimes called tip cuttings. The end or tip of the stem is cut off to a length of about 6-9 cm (2½-3½ in), and will produce roots at the injury, provided this is made immediately below a leaf joint.

Stoloniferous: of plants, producing shoots, buds or stems from the base of the plant.

Stomachic: substance which strengthens and tones the stomach, and often counteracts or relieves cramps.

Tea: solution made by pouring boiling water on to the fermented leaves and stems of a plant which have been allowed to dry after fermentation. Pour about 150 ml/¼ pint/⅔ cup on to a teaspoonful of dried material, let the liquid stand for between 3 to 10 minutes and then serve.

Theophrastus: (born 370 B.C.) Greek philosopher and pupil of both Aristotle and Plato, who wrote a botanical survey of plants called an *Enquiry into Plants*. It is the earliest of the surviving books on plants written about Mediterranean, as well as Indian, Egyptian and Arabian, species. Theophrastus allegedly lived to the age of 107.

Thymol: an antiseptic phenol or acid obtained from oil of thyme by distillation.

Tip: of cuttings, describes those taken from the youngest stems, sometimes also called 'soft' cuttings.

Tisane: solution made in a similar way to tea but differing from it in that fresh or dried, rather than fermented, green leaves and stems are used. Add about 150 ml/¼ pint/⅔ cup of boiling water to either 1 teaspoon of dried material, or 2-3 of fresh, and take without milk, although a little honey may be added.

Toothed: describes the margin of a leaf which is evenly cut into sections; sometimes also called dentate.

Trefoil: three-fold; a clover leaf is a trefoil leaf with three leaflets.

Umbel: cluster of flowers whose stems radiate from a central point on the main stem like an upturned umbrella, the flower-stems all being the same length so that the 'umbrella' is flat-topped. In the plant family *Umbelliferae* all the flowerheads have this form.

Vermifuge: substance which expels or destroys intestinal worms.

Viable: alive or able to live; of plants, a seed which still has the capacity to germinate.

Index

ACKNOWLEDGEMENTS
The publishers would like to thank the following individuals and organizations for their help in producing this book:
Culpeper Ltd; Simon Danischewsky; Elizabeth Hunt; David Mellor Ltd, 4 Sloane Square, London SW3.

Picture credits
Harry Smith Collection 11; A-Z Botanical 12, 13, 14; Harry Smith Collection 15(3); Tania Midgley 17; Harry Smith 18; Bruce Coleman 19 (top 2); Iris Hardwick 19(2); Bruce Coleman 21; Iris Hardwick 23; Harry Smith 24 (top); Iris Hardwick 24 (centre); A-Z Botanical 24; Harry Smith 25; Tania Midgley 27; Bruce Coleman 29; Harry Smith 30; Bruce Coleman 33; Tania Midgley 35; A-Z Botanical 37; Tania Midgley 38; Harry Smith 39; A-Z Botanical 115; Harry Smith 116; Bruce Coleman 117(2); MacClancy Collection 119; Paget Joseph 121, 122, 123; Bruce Coleman 125, 126(2); Iris Hardwick 127; Bruce Coleman 128.